# Out of the Dark

# Out of the Dark

A Direction for Change in Education

WENDY L. SAMFORD

Foreword by William F. Pinar

RESOURCE *Publications* • Eugene, Oregon

OUT OF THE DARK
A Direction for Change in Education

Copyright © 2016 Wendy L. Samford. All rights reserved. Except for brief quotations in critical publications or reviews, no part of this book may be reproduced in any manner without prior written permission from the publisher. Write: Permissions, Wipf and Stock Publishers, 199 W. 8th Ave., Suite 3, Eugene, OR 97401.

Resource Publications
An Imprint of Wipf and Stock Publishers
199 W. 8th Ave., Suite 3
Eugene, OR 97401

www.wipfandstock.com

PAPERBACK ISBN: 978-1-4982-8116-4
HARDCOVER ISBN: 978-1-4982-8118-8
EBOOK ISBN: 978-1-4982-8117-1

Manufactured in the U.S.A.   06/30/16

God for His unending direction of my paths
My husband Scott and my children; Addie, Joe, Savannah, and Evan for their unwavering support
Book club members, you know who you are
All teachers

# Contents

*Foreword by William F. Pinar* | ix
*Introduction* | xiii

1 **Standards and Standardization** | 1
2 **Freedom from Oppression** | 22
3 **Sustaining Change** | 36
4 **The Vastness of Curriculum Development** | 53
5 **A Platform for Curriculum Development** | 71
6 **Renewal** | 91
7 **A Call for Action** | 109

*Bibliography* | 125

# Foreword

When does the futures become *now*? Is the "opt-out" movement the "spark for exodus from controlled, mandated curriculum," (92) deliverance into a time when, Wendy Samford wonders, "teachers take responsibility for curriculum development in their building, all on the cutting edge of information, improving professional knowledge?" (52). Educators in the United States have been waiting for such a future longer than most can remember, as Samford appreciates. She provides a history of the present, plagued as it is by "teaching to the test, student cheating, [shift of] control of curriculum from educators to organizations, and harmful levels of stress" (20). Referencing the "opt-out" movement she acknowledges that "a growing number of parents and teachers are questioning standards and evaluation of those standards," (62) but she insists "that more of us in the field of education need to inquire and push for deliberation about curriculum" (62). Why? "If teachers are not seeing, interpreting, and questioning curriculum," Samford explains, "it is perceived by those outside of the field as acceptance" (62).

This is but one insight in this book, this "spark" that could start an exodus, to remember our common faith, to renew the nation. "We, educators," Samford writes, "must begin to assert ourselves in making the statement that we are the professionals in our field" (14). In a time when everything is politicized, this sentence could be misread by some as an assertion of self-interest. It—and many stirring sentences that precede and follow it—is an

## Foreword

affirmation of professional judgment, yes technical know-how but also "wisdom." "Curriculum wisdom," Samford clarifies, "focuses on cultivating values that endure the test of time. It requires the absolute commitment to asking the tough questions about content; such questions are deep with meaning about generosity, compassion, the good of all, who benefits, what does our community believe, will it last, does it make the world a better place?" (66). These are the professional—curricular—questions many educators used to ask, when they were left to contemplate the awesome often overwhelming responsibility to educate the young.

For some sixty years' educators have had no time to contemplate the meanings—personal or public—of their work, as they have been victimized by an ongoing manufactured crisis concocted first during the Cold War, then tied the globalization of the economy, now obsessed with test scores, providing political ammunition for private corporations to sell schools their wares. "As we educators lead the renewal of our schools" Samford knows, to think instead about "renewal," and specifically "to re-think what we know about and how we understand curriculum development" (62).

Samford provides such a Platform for Curriculum Development (PCD), a platform that is like a garden: "creating a platform for change is very much like a making a garden. We work to clear the area of debris and move on to tilling the soil, laying the groundwork for growth. Seeds must then be planted and cared for regularly. However, there is no certainty that the seeds will grow and the garden will flourish" (73). Quantified outcomes are illusory; ethical aspirations are not. Ethics not economics animate teachers' engagement with the young in their midst.

"We must take an active role in the future of education," Samford admonishes her beleaguered colleagues, "we must work together to be living examples of democracy for our students" (xx). Knowledge informs action, and she pleads: "Arm yourself with information. Take offense at the standardization requirements you are being forced to implement on a regular basis. Think about the affects of standardization on this generation's ability to create, originate, formulate and design ideas for the future." (xxi)

## Foreword

Autobiographical, theoretical, historical, and heartfelt, *Out of the Dark* is a powerful—reverberating—appeal of one educator to her colleagues: "Take a stand, lock arms and join in; the time is now" (xxi). Yes, the future is now.

William F. Pinar

# Introduction

I recently resigned my position as an administrator of thirteen years. The "calling" to write this book has been building for some time, but quite honestly, I was afraid. It is hard to leave an occupation for reasons of principle, to jump ship when others seem to be able to endure. I have four children, and I watch as the two youngest are pummeled with the pervasive culture of testing in education that is irresponsible and unnecessary. After years of working very hard to educate myself, I left my career and it was one of the most difficult decisions I have had to make.

Before leaving, I was taking an active part in the current support and encouragement of this present day regurgitation of a mandated curriculum. Curriculum that teachers have very little control over. To watch as teachers are forced to transmit a nationally directed, but privately financed prescribed curriculum, is no longer something that I can associate myself with ethically. I find myself in a query as to how I can contribute to a field that I have spent a lifetime gathering experience and education; a field in which I no longer "fit."

This book is an extension of the edited book *Reconceptualizing Curriculum Development*.[1] I was one of twenty practitioners that shared their knowledge and elaborated on their journeys to live as democratic educators.[2] Through participating in this process, I knew that I was not alone in the belief that curriculum

---

1. Henderson et al., *Reconceptualizing Curriculum Development*.
2. Pinar, *What is Curriculum Theory*.

## Introduction

development is the responsibility of every educator. Through this collaborative experience, I knew I had to contribute more than one chapter[3] to this calling, and more specifically, I felt compelled to share my ideas with my colleagues in this field, those I know and those I may never meet. I felt the need to write what I have learned and share experiences of teachers that have so drastically touched my life, that continue to fight the fight in classrooms every day, weary as they may be. This book is a call for teachers to band together against the misrepresentation of standardized management as the prominent paradigm today. It is a plea for educators to finally say, "This is not right, and we do not philosophically agree with the hypocrisy of the educational system as it currently exists!" This book is for teachers, those in classrooms and those wearing administrative shoes; educators who know there is a better way to democratically educate children. The purpose of this book is twofold. Firstly, this book provides teachers with information so they feel empowered to take a stand united against the standardized management paradigm in which they find themselves today, and secondly, this book offers information to support curriculum development when the above initiative is successful. The many references throughout this book were used deliberately so that teachers have many options for supportive reading when they begin their journey.

Our nation's children and young adults are being taught directed subject matter, over tested on content, and then labeled on the outcome. So much of a teacher's valuable time is spent on helping kids understand the test questions, content that was previously valued is set aside, and critical conversation about curriculum development is practically ignored. I have seen teachers cut units that empower their students with worthwhile, thought provoking information in order to fit content into a federally prescribed standard. In doing so, teachers skip valuable ingredients that encompass a holistic education. We live in a time where there is very little tolerance for deviation from the standards if you want

---

3. Samford, "Deliberative Conversation."

# Introduction

an evaluation that will elicit a proficient rating, the "passing" label you can expect on your ability scale.

A mandated standardized management paradigm that does not allow for deviation from over tested content is not ethical. This restrictive paradigm we are witnessing begs the critical question: What is the "right" way to educate our children? This question has been argued way before the *McGuffey's Eclectic Primer*[4] came to town in a horse drawn buggy and continues through today's twisted form of Tyler's[5] rationale with a rote, pre-formatted outline for lesson plans allowing little wiggle room for curriculum "development." I offer a few suggested priorities in the education of our children that I think many people can agree upon.

1. We need to be able to have the ability to comprehend in multimodal ways and articulate our intent. To quote the contemporary American educational philosopher, Maxine Greene, "We have to be articulate enough and able to exert ourselves to name what we see around us."[6] This quote supports articulation at least minimally at the level in which we want to insert ourselves into the world. For example, if someone's goal is to become a craftsman in a chosen field, he/she must be proficient at comprehending written direction for using a new tool, and be adept with fine-motor skills to use the equipment, thus creating harmony between written direction and actual practice. If, however, someone desires to be an engineer, his/her literature may be scientifically based and formal schooling would be very different than in a skilled profession. The value of articulation does not in any way lessen the impact of all subjects including mathematics, social studies, science, or the arts,[7] guiding us on our ability to impact our world. Simply stated, reading is a primary color on our educational pallet.

---

4. McGuffey, *McGuffey's Eclectic Primer.*
5. Tyler, *Basic Principles of Curriculum and Instruction.*
6. Greene, *Releasing the Imagination,* 111.
7. Eisner, *Kind of Schools We Need.*

## INTRODUCTION

2. We need to understand that we are but a part of the whole. Although we each have individual needs, we all have an innate need to be a part of something bigger than ourselves. Socrates way of thinking was to be an advocate for our own happiness with a deep concern for others.[8] This outlook promotes a safeguard for the welfare of others through constant communication that strives to make the best choices for our happiness as well as the overall betterment of others. Of course, the argument can be made that try as we may, we do not always make decisions for the betterment of the whole, but that aside, deep down we all want to be a part of a bigger truth than that of our own.

3. Someone needs to lead instruction. According to Dewey, not only are the "mature" supposed to guide instruction, but they also have the "responsibility" to do so.[9] "The present affects the future anyway. The persons who should have some idea of the connection between the two are those who have achieved maturity. Accordingly, upon them devolves the responsibility for instituting the conditions for the kind of present experience which has a favorable effect upon the future."[10] For purposes of this book, those mature mentors with a sense of responsibility are teachers. We, teachers, can impact the present for our students and ourselves in turn shaping future generations.

The time has come to stop thinking about school reform—politically lead short-term goals that fly in with flocks of politicians. Instead, we need to seek school renewal,[11] which demands continuous critical inquiry focusing on the process of sustained change in education. Renewal, as opposed to reform, elicits the collegiality of educators working together to improve practice, while finding ways to connect their lives and the lives of those

8. Palmer, *Fifty Modern Thinkers on Education.*
9. Dewey, *Experience & Education*, 50.
10. Ibid., 50.
11. Sirotnik, "Making Sense of Educational Renewal," 606–610.

INTRODUCTION

they influence; renewal embraces democracy in its truest sense.[12] This renewal of education requires re-thinking how we develop curriculum that embraces subject, self, and social understanding[13] in order to support a forward movement away from the tyranny in which we find ourselves.[14] There is no doubt that change is difficult,[15] but this call to arms is for those ready to dig into the present by taking a hard look at standardization[16] while discovering the freedom[17] that comes with forging new possibilities. It is my hope that together, we begin answering Pinar, Reynolds, Slattery, and Taubman's[18] call for discovering the past while applying the theories we already know, thus forging together to develop new philosophies supporting and sustaining the change needed in education today. Let us commit to the present challenge of informing curriculum development through a platform created specifically for professional development dedicated to exposing the present, envisioning the past, and supporting the journey[19] that committed individuals will undergo as a result of this empowering renewal.

## CHAPTER 1: STANDARDS AND STANDARDIZATION

How did the all-consuming standardization of education happen? I have been asked this question repeatedly by teachers who are truly at a loss as to how we became engulfed in a standardized management paradigm at an alarmingly fast and all-inclusive manner. This chapter provides a good overview of standardization in public education including the politically supported privatization of a

---

12. Nancy, *Truth of Democracy*.
13. Henderson and Gornik, *Transformative Curriculum Leadership*.
14. Watkins, *Assault on Public Education*.
15. Kegan, *Evolving Self, In Over Our Heads, Immunity to Change*.
16. Bell and Peters, *We Make the Road by Walking*.
17. Greene, *Dialectic of Freedom*.
18. Pinar et al., *Understanding Curriculum*.
19. Pinar, *What is Curriculum Theory*.

*INTRODUCTION*

previously public enterprise, namely our schools. The chapter begs two questions: 1) How did we get here? alongside 2) Do we truly believe we are teaching in the manner we philosophically support?

## CHAPTER 2: FREEDOM FROM OPPRESSION

Whether perceived or a reality, teachers are being held back from providing democratic education for all students. Simultaneously, outside forces continue to constrain educators' professional growth. This chapter delves into theories behind oppression while exploring what it looks like in education today and why teachers find themselves in a state of oppression. Chapter 2 begs the question: How are we motivated to break out of an oppressive cycle towards freedom? Ultimately, this chapter stresses that emancipation from an oppressive state must first come from the realization that we are, in fact, oppressed. Once recognized, it is our duty to break free and look for the empowerment that we seek, including our students' rights to a holistic education.

## CHAPTER 3: SUSTAINING CHANGE

This chapter presents theories of change, an interpretation of the motivation behind change, and a guideline to initiating and sustaining change. Changing one's mindset is critical for the support of sustained change, a change in beliefs and in practices. I use Ryan's[20] interpretation of the Dewey and Bentley's circuit of inquiry[21] to illuminate the cycle of change. Change occurs when nonreflective experience is disrupted by a problem that one's common habits cannot supply the solution to. Thus, the problem prompts the development of a hypothesis and one uses tools and data to test the hypothesis until the object (a return to nonreflectivity) is reached. This theory of change is specifically poignant if teachers are to break the cycle of habit and realize that there is a problem,

20. Ryan, *Seeing Together*.
21. Dewey and Bentley, *Knowing and the Known*.

INTRODUCTION

that is, the over standardization of public education today. Realization of this problem initiates action and prompts change. Change does not come without conflict, which should be embraced with resolutions in place to address confrontation when it occurs.

## CHAPTER 4: THE VASTNESS OF CURRICULUM DEVELOPMENT

A discussion of negotiating and crossing between the paradigms of standardized management and of curriculum wisdom is explored through curriculum development. This chapter looks at past curriculum theory and is a call for teachers to become lead learners taking responsibility for their own journeys. The chapter encourages educators to incorporate curriculum wisdom into the pre-existing standardized system and introduces a 3S curriculum design,[22] the integration of subject matter understanding with democratic self and social understanding. This chapter does not intend to discount the need for assessment or the documentation of data but refutes standardization as the dominant means by which to do so. Chapter 4 promotes embarking on a journey that informs action for the development of a curriculum wisdom paradigm in our current educational system.

## CHAPTER 5: A PLATFORM FOR CURRICULUM DEVELOPMENT

In order to construct democratic curriculum created with and by colleagues, a Platform for Curriculum Development[23] needs to be established to support complicated conversation about curriculum and pedagogy with oneself and others.[24] A Platform for Curriculum Development elicits administrative support to make time to develop trust thus promoting collegiality that expects sustained

22. Henderson and Gornik, *Transformative Curriculum Leadership.*
23. Samford, "Exploring Sustained Change," 27–44.
24. Pinar, *What is Curriculum Theory.*

change grounded in democratic values to support curriculum development. This chapter recognizes a platform must be developed in the school environment to support sustaining change.

## CHAPTER 6: RENEWAL

Offering insights and illustrations for change, chapter 6 presents schools that have taken on the challenge of school renewal. Various examples of schools that have created their own rendition of a democratic school setting are explored. Theirs is a hermeneutic compilation of creative curriculum development embracing a collegial, empowering environment. From examples of schools that honor a natural approach of choice to campuses that completely encapsulate empowering their teachers with professional development, this chapter delves into the current theory of design and management of schools that work to facilitate creative, collegial, and reflective curriculum development.

## CHAPTER 7: A CALL FOR ACTION

The final chapter is a challenge for all educators to begin to empower themselves with information to become informed advocates for the creation of a democratic platform for curriculum development. We must take an active role in the future of education, and we must work together as lead learners, as active participants who are living examples of democracy for our students. Chapter 7 is call for teachers to arm themselves with information and begin to communicate with each other in an open dialogue to discuss the purpose of education.

I believe we are in an oppressive time in education. It is a time when we are being held hostage with an over tested, mandated curriculum that negatively effects public education. Let us together revisit the educational philosophies that helped establish this great nation and move forward in a democratic dialogue of curriculum development for, with, and by the people that are in

## INTRODUCTION

the field of education. Arm yourself with information. Take offense at the standardization requirements you are being forced to implement on a regular basis. Begin thinking critically about the affects of standardization on generations of students' abilities to create, originate, formulate, and design ideas for the future. Continuously fight for your right to have a work environment where support for curriculum development is a necessary ingredient for empowerment in the field of education. Take a stand, lock arms, and join in; the time is now.

# 1

# Standards and Standardization

"Before real change can occur, we have to clear a space where we can take stock of where we are and how we arrived here."[1]

How can we join together and create a plan to move forward if we do not know how we arrived at this standardized management paradigm in education? How did this happen? How did we get here? We think we are somewhat politically attuned with the times because we watch television and read the newspaper. I have concluded that the politics of standardization is a study unto itself. Just as we are experts in the field of education, there are experts in the field of politics. I struggled with the topic of standardization in public education, wondering if it was too much information for one chapter and if I could do the topic justice. However, the fact remains, too many educators are not able to articulate in a concise, informed manner how we arrived in a standardized management paradigm. This chapter is designed to help answer that question.

Differentiating between standards and standardization is important. Standards are used to give curriculum a content

1. Taubman, *Teaching by Numbers*, x.

direction. Although most teachers I have talked to do not like the fact that standards are dictated, the fact remains, educators have always followed some type of standards to illustrate a desired course or direction. Standardization, for purposes of this book, is a paradigm we are witnessing today with over-indulgence on the importance of accountability measured solely by standardized evaluations. Standardized evaluations are short sighted, restraining, and prohibitive. They promote complacency. Nationally-mandated standards coupled with over dependency on testing are part of the standardized management paradigm we are witnessing. This chapter looks at standards, standardization, and government intervention promoting the over reliance on accountability based solely on standardization. My hope is that this chapter presents some of the history behind the present state of public education.

We have been reduced to a position of producing numbers that we are forced to extract from children, both willing and resistant, in order to receive a proficient evaluation score. The value that is placed on ratings in schools is insurmountable which, in turn, adds unrealistic amounts of pressure on teachers held responsible for this rating. I sat on the panel for a teacher candidate recently where an already struggling interviewee was asked a question in which she answered, "Well this may not be the popular answer, but I don't believe in all this testing." You could hear crickets chirping while the interview team sat uncomfortably, shifting in their seats. Had she, in a public forum, addressed the topic of which we do not speak? Did she voice an opposing position to that of standardized testing? I tried to help out the recent graduate by saying, "I believe any one of us would be hard pressed to find a teacher that disagreed with you." Heads nodded in agreement until, much to my dismay, another administrator retorted, "You know that Dr. Samford and I have children. They depend upon us for their livelihood, their food, their clothing. Our jobs depend upon you doing your job of scoring well on the achievement tests. Tell me how you are going to score well on the tests; our children's very existence depends on it." It is not likely that this candidate was going to get the position; noticeably, the philosophical variance was too extreme. I use this example not to pick on administrators — I was one for thirteen years — but simply to illustrate the deeply rooted over-importance of testing results engrained in our public school systems.

## STANDARDS

Currently in the United States, forty-three states have adopted *Common Core State Standards*.[2] A quick search can reveal many articles with strong views about the multiple controversies over these standards. For instance, North Dakota has a website dedicated to banning these standards with simple instructions on how to contact the House Judiciary Committee to vote yes on HB1461, which would ban these standards in their state.[3] Interestingly, on this same website are step-by-step instructions on how to get started nullifying these standards in your own state. A major complaint about the *Common Core Standards* includes the level of difficulty that is not developmentally acceptable. Contrasting is the definition of "standards" in the dictionary represented as "a level of quality, achievement, etc., that is considered acceptable or desirable."[4]

When I began in this profession as a teacher, we had curriculum guides created by teachers in the school district. There were standards, paths to follow outlining objectives, behavior, and content probably following the Tyler rationale whereas the teacher "can provide an educational experience through setting up an environment and structuring the situation so as to simulate the desired type of reaction."[5] I then remember being a very green administrator, working collaboratively with teachers to create curriculum maps to better understand the *Academic Content Standards*.[6] And today, we are forced to follow the *Common Core State Standards*,[7]

2. Common Core State Standards Initiative, "Standards in your State," 1.
3. Trejo, "North Dakota Action Alert."
4. Merriam Webster Dictionary, "standard."
5. Tyler, *Basic Principles,* 64.
6. Ohio Department of Education, "Academic Content Standards Extended."
7. Ibid.

just another label for nationally norm-referenced standards mandated and supported through federal grants. Tracing the transition from locally created curriculum to a national agenda is fairly easy. Nonetheless, we have always followed some type of standard, whether our own or one that is currently mandated.

I remember walking into my first classroom and asking what curriculum I was supposed to follow. The general business class I taught was an elective with no curriculum. So, I could order textbooks and teach what content I thought was best. The school was on a block schedule model, which gave me ninety-minutes to teach the objectives of business to sophomore high school students. It was the best time I have ever had in a classroom, we learned and grew together, all of us. Still, I used the book as an outline for the content of the class. One could argue that the standards I used in the class were based on those of the publisher. What ever the guide may be, teachers use some standards that people in a discipline's field believe are important to know and learn. This, of course, does not mean that curriculum resides only in a textbook or that objectives equate the total sum of learning experiences. However, whether teachers obtain content information from a curriculum guide or textbook and eventually materials gathered from experience, we have all used resources as some form of outline to initially guide our courses. The point being standards are not the enemy.

Teachers are not afraid of standards, but the over reliance on nationally-mandated curriculum for the sole purpose of evaluation is wrong. One teacher I spoke with recently shared, "I'm not afraid of the Core standards because I am established, I know where to add what really needs to be taught in my grade level, the background information kids need to truly understand the concept. What scares me are the new teachers in the field that are only focused on standards because they have no prior experience. How do they know what is missing?" Good question. Teachers no longer have local control of adding information or more importantly, removing information from their curriculum. All control of content is mandated by national standards where there was a "virtual absence of classroom teacher participation in the group developing the standards" but well represented were the "testing industry and special-interest groups."[8] Sadly, as I write this, I received an email from one of my children's teachers about the homework for the night with a disclaimer at the bottom, "Please know that I am teaching these concepts how the state is asking that they be taught." Howard Gardner[9] would challenge the present assumption that people learn the same material in the same way. According to Gardner, society would be better served if teachers could present subjects in a number of ways and learning assessed through a variety of formats. The opposite of Gardner's research is true with standardization.

## STANDARDIZATION

Merriam-Webster Dictionary[10] defines standardize as "to compare with a standard" or "to bring into conformity with a standard." Interestingly there are two examples given to help understand the definition. The first example is about business "He standardized procedures for the industry." The second example is about education "The plan is to standardize the test for reading comprehension so that we can see how students across the state compare." The irony is alarming.

Quantifying a standard requires conformity in order to evaluate the results. Teachers are now required to conduct data analysis using pre-tests, post-tests, formative testing, and summative testing. In Ohio, for example, the Educational Service Center assists to disseminate information from the State Support Team to conduct the Ohio Improvement Process. All schools in Ohio are required to go through some form of this process. Although the initiative has merit for professional development by inviting central office personnel, building administrators, and teachers to collaborate, the push for standardization of goals is ever present.

8. Hoover, "PARCC and Common Core," 1.
9. Gardner, *Frames of Mind*.
10. Merriam Webster Dictionary, "standardize."

One teacher confided, "Initially, I was really excited to be chosen for the committee. I thought I could really contribute, but after two evening meetings of constructive brainstorming, the objectives were directed to us and they were all about the report card." Now, teachers must "prove" gains in their classrooms. One teacher quipped, "If they are giving me a scripted curriculum, why are they evaluating me? Isn't the test evaluating the script?"

In the standardized management movement and with the added responsibility of additional testing and data analysis, little time is left for diagnostic intervention. An established teacher whispered to me in the hallway of her aversion to giving the last of three pre-tests that were required in her class. The final test was to be given after the state assessment and the teacher did not understand the reasoning. In the past, teachers would joke, "Tests are over, now we can teach!" Are we now fully compliant to national conformity whether we are testing or not? This is especially questionable if the purpose for the data collected is to aggregate data for statistical reasoning. Such drive toward uniformity and standardization regardless of individual interests and the judgments of the educators in various subject areas creates a clear danger and causes stress, even suffering.[11] We should not be reliant on standardization as the only measurement of the success of our students.

Not even addressed in this chapter is the duress that children are under because of the tests.[12] We know that the standardization of public schools is causing our kids undue stress; we can see it on a daily basis. The data collected needs to be questioned as to the validity of the conditions under which kids are tested. "Fundamentally, tests provide little more than data, but just as one must question the confessions extracted under torture, one has to wonder just how reliable that data is, when it is wrung out of students shocked by the constant administration of tests."[13] If kids can get past the anxiety and receive a proficient score, federal mandates

---

11. Pignatelli, "Everyday Courage in the Midst of Standardization in Schools," 230–235.

12. McDonald, "Prevalence and Effects of Test Anxiety," 89–101.

13. Taubman, *Teaching by Numbers*, 28.

dictate that the bar be raised yearly and the very same score is no longer considered proficient. This arbitrary line in the sand is washed away and new goals are set.

Nine years ago I was analyzing data used to identify our gifted population when I noticed that our scores dropped dramatically in overall performance. Baring the theory that we all suddenly dropped in IQ in one town in Ohio, I dug deeper into the Cognitive Abilities Test (CogAT) to find the norming criteria that year had been changed. They sold us on the new test, adding color and some pictures, but we did not realize that the norming had been adjusted as well. We had not gotten dumber. Apparently, the criteria on which we were being compared was adjusted. The line mysteriously erased and was re-calculated behind statistical closed doors. In 2012, another example of creating illusions to support invisible standardization goals occurred when the Ohio Department of Education added STAR Math Enterprise and STAR Reading Enterprise (i.e., a Renaissance product on the state-supported vendors list) to the list of approved assessments for gifted identification. These are not nationally normed tests but boast that they predict achievement. As of February, 2014, after a vast over-identification of gifted students had taken place, the STAR tests were mysteriously removed. It is hard when you are being tossed around in a quagmire of statistical gaming without a controller. Statistics are easy to manipulate and when we allow outside forces to control curriculum priorities in public education, we become exposed to their agenda, whatever that may be. So who is controlling our curriculum?

## GOVERNMENT INTERVENTION

The strangle hold that standardized management has on our public school systems cannot be overstated, and politics is entangled in its roots. The agenda of politics in education is not new,[14] but the current political invasion of a previously local agenda is increasingly

14. Bobbitt, *The Curriculum*. Kliebard, *Struggle for American Curriculum*.

alarming. Political infiltration of this magnitude is not something we have previously witnessed in education. "Its uniqueness lies in its pervasiveness, its threat to the very foundations of public education, its wide embrace by the educational establishment, its direct assault on the intellectual, aesthetic and ethical life of teachers, and its radical misunderstanding of teaching."[15]

When did the government get involved in education? An interesting article credits the entry of a national influence into education through a federal commission charged with investigating "Life Adjustment for Youth"[16] as early as 1954. This commission was to look at education for appropriate learning experiences, educating for living and livelihood, values, and moral living. Although many have focused on *No Child Left Behind*[17] for the national influx into public schools, the first time education is mentioned in a national legislation was the *National Defense Education Act of 1958*.[18] President Eisenhower targeted schools to increase the number of mathematicians to support growth of technology in the United States. Sputnik was launched the year prior causing panic and an overwhelming perception that the United States was behind in the space race. In 1983, *A Nation at Risk*[19] was published having a monumental impact on education. This report called for national involvement to supplement state, local, and other resources to support specific national goals for education and asked for people, civic groups, and businesses to volunteer and get involved in order to strengthen the quality of education. This document elicited that we were indeed behind other nations, therefore at risk, and that the federal government should have the primary responsibility of identifying the national interest of our educational system.

15. Taubman, *Teaching by Numbers*, 5.
16. Janet, "Life Adjustment," 137–141.
17. U.S. Department of Education, "No Child Left Behind."
18. U.S. Department of Education, "Elementary and Secondary Education Act."
19. U.S. Department of Education, "A Nation at Risk."

## Standards and Standardization

But were we really at risk? Today, when we break apart the test information, taking into account race and poverty level, we glean a different perspective.

> When data are stratified by income level, the average score for schools with more than half of their students above poverty level is above the U.S. average score and far above the international average score. When data are broken down by race and then compared with the average scores, U.S. white students repeatedly score in the top five internationally for the 25 to 30 industrial countries studies, while Black and Latino students repeatedly score in the bottom five.[20]

The public panic that *A Nation at Risk* intended to elicit and the response that it received prompted twenty years of fear that our country was falling behind other nations globally.

In the 1990s, venture capitalism began to enter the scene supported by the technology boom, which pushed privatization and helped initiate the stronghold of the government in education today. In 2002, President Bush reauthorized the *Elementary and Secondary Education Act*[21] calling it, *No Child Left Behind* (Public Law PL 107–110).[22] The legislation passed through Congress with bipartisan support. As quite well known now, NCLB supports a standards-based curriculum and mandates measurable goals in order for schools to receive any federal funding. The law greatly increased the participation and integration of the national role in public education and began an extremely negative campaign against the teaching profession.

In 2003, the Teaching Commission was created to focus on teacher quality. The purpose of this commission, which consisted of big business leaders and politicians, was to offer recommendations for policies to ensure student learning. The commission was clear to point out that protection of teachers in their profession was to be looked at as a priority for restructuring; teacher evaluation was

---

20. Gerson, "Neoliberal Agenda," 103.
21. Ibid.
22. Ibid.

targeted. The report that was created as a result of this commission was entitled, *Teaching at Risk; A Call to Action*,[23] and called for a targeted campaign to revamp the profession of teaching. Wanted was a different type of teacher recruited into the field of education in order to restructure public schools. Following shortly thereafter, *The Secretary's Third Annual Report of Teacher Quality* used statements such as "what was good enough for previous generations is not sufficient today and woefully inadequate for the future" and "our high school students lag behind other students."[24]

In 2007 the National Center on Education and the Economy (NCEE), which was and is completely funded by philanthropists and corporate business, produced a report that labeled the old system of education unable to be fixed supporting the need for a new public system of education.[25] Testing is central to the NCEE's restructuring of the old public school system including a mandatory universal exam to provide comparison statistics that decide who is capable of advancing to higher education opportunities. Suddenly, there were two distinct characteristics of reform: 1) excellence is defined as proficient math and reading test scores and 2) standardization is the means to achieve this excellence.[26] "Reform is really a misnomer because the advocates for this cause seek not to reform public education but to transform it into an entrepreneurial sector of the economy."[27] Diane Ravitch believes that with the newest incentives, "This is the first time in history that the U.S. Department of Education designed programs with the intent of stimulating private sector investors to create for-profit ventures in American education."[28]

What were we, in the field of education doing while all this transpired? The teachers' unions had a clear choice; break with the

23. Education Commission, "Teaching at Risk."

24. U.S. Department of Education, "Secretary's Third Annual Report of Teacher Quality," 2.

25. Watkins, "New Social Order," 27.

26. Zhao, *Catching Up or Leading the Way*, 1–63.

27. Ravitch, *Reign of Error*, 19.

28. Ibid., 17.

politics of education and resist the push for standardization or find a place where they could agree with corporate reform and assimilate. The unions chose to conform.[29] Rather than taking a stance, the National Education Association remained quiet on most issues, electing to assist in policy verbiage and help with the creation of state and then national standards.[30] Where were our school boards? A national poll of school board members in 2011 showed a distinct change in focus from buildings, budgets, books, and so on to school performance, teacher evaluations, and charter schools.[31] Although resistance to the funneling of money to charter schools was publicized, ultimately communities settled into conformity. Calling schools "Excellent" looks good on a banner and striving for that distinction became the suburban norm, meanwhile our urban schools struggled to keep the neoliberal agenda from continually closing schools with no community voice.[32]

## NEOLIBERALISM

Neoliberalism is a form of economics where power shifts from the public into the private sector. Very simply stated, neoliberalism removes barriers and regulations allowing a laissez-faire attitude for economic development. One of the many effects of neoliberalism in education is the vast control that business elicits over educational reforms and policies. Neoliberalism grays distinctions between political parties and joins private corporations in expanding capitalism globally. Thus, we see the "every man for himself" mentality witnessed today as opposed to our declarations of a democratic social structure. Our economy has developed a new social order based on money. "The richest 1% of adults own 40% of the world's assets, the richest 2% of adults own 50% of the world's assets and the richest 10% of adults own 85% of the world's

---

29. Gerson, "Neoliberal Agenda," 97–124.
30. Sawchuk, "NEA Proposes," 18–19.
31. Samuels, "Survey Detects Shifting," 22.
32. Lipman, "Neoliberal Urbanism," 33–54.

assets."[33] Moreover, "the wealthiest 10% of the U.S. population now own nine-tenths of all stocks."[34] Our government sold public education out to the private sector as un-tapped revenue. They contrived an agenda that consisted of "condemning the schools, manufacturing a crisis, starving public schools of resources, standardizing curriculum and teaching methods, and opening up education to for-profit companies."[35] Collectively, the belief system of this new social order is that public schools must be measured in order to show a return on a quite sizable investment. This is a business model that intends to produce workers and consumers that are competitive in a global market. According to Taubman, the leading proponents of educational reform today are venture philanthropists including the Bill and Melinda Gates Foundation, the Eli and Edythe Broad Foundation, and the Walton Family Foundation. Advertised as promoting public good for reform and remedies, they were instrumental in promoting school choice and incentive pay as well as and most recently, quantitatively measuring venture capitals investment in schools.

For example, the Eli and Edythe Broad Foundation has focused much of their attention on transforming public schools by targeting administration.[36] This foundation proposes bad management causes the problems in public education and strongly supports standardized testing. The Broad Foundation supports Data Partnership (i.e., a subset of the School Information Partnership), which targets compiling and analyzing test scores to influence school education policy. In this partnership, "the U.S. Department of Education provided $4.7 million and $50.9 million came from private organizations. Of this, Broad provided half."[37] We, teachers and other educational stakeholders, need to begin recognizing who is behind the push for standardized management and start asking critical questions about money dictating who chooses curriculum

33. Watkins, "New Social Order," 10.
34. Ibid., 11.
35. Taubman, *Teaching by Numbers*, 104.
36. Saltman, "Rise of Venture Philanthropy," 211–225.
37. Ibid., 73.

and assessments. When we allow philanthropists to dictate the direction of our curriculum and teaching the concern becomes, "efficient enforcement of the "right" knowledge, critical engagement, investigation, and intellectual curiosity, not to mention cultural and class differences, appear as impediments to learning, as teachers are treated as deskilled deliverers of prepackaged curricula, prohibiting their potential as critical intellectuals."[38] When we permit outside private business to standardize our schools, it prohibits the "kinds of questioning, critical dialogue and tools of investigation necessary for fostering of democratic culture that citizens must learn in order to participate in reworking civil society with others."[39] Influence begins to be outside of the community and local ideals and local customs and priorities are lost to business agendas.

I am reminded of a special education team meeting I attended several years ago that included the teachers, the guidance counselor, an administrator, and the parents of the student. The Individualized Education Plan (IEP) forms had changed, again, and we were reviewing the new section entitled Post-Secondary Transition. The section mandates that special education teachers test their students on their skills for targeted occupations and then combine that information with the student's future wishes. A scripted dialogue narrates what a twelve/thirteen-year-old student must work toward for their future, allowing no room for change and completely age inappropriate. How many thirteen-year-olds know what they want to be when they grow up? When I was thirteen, I wanted to live in a commune with my best friend Mara and raise animals. Just try to formally dictate a child's occupational goals when "Johnny" wants to be a baseball player. I remember the embarrassment I felt when one of the teachers was forced to read a script beginning with "Johnny will. . ." about career goals that may or may not ever be attained. Witnessing this scripted reading showcases that in education we are losing our ability to engage in rich debate and high level discussion. Put another way,

38. Ibid, 59.
39. Ibid, 62.

our educational deliberations are slipping away. Deliberation lies at the very heart of the concept of a team where you can choose what to say together based on the best–and most realistic–plan for each student. Now, a script is dictated for fear from looming litigation and the consequences from it.

Why have we, as a democratic society, allowed private enterprise to be empowered with the ability to determine what we value in education? How does a billionaire philanthropist have more expertise and a better idea of how children learn than we, as educational professionals, do? Are we ready to say after pondering, arguing, creating, and adjusting curriculum theory for centuries that we are saved by private business entrepreneurs deciding what students need to know and learn? There are major problems in the assumed ability of business entrepreneurs to cross over into the field of education and be successful. One main problem of this transfer of authority is simple; business is for profit not to mention increasing competitiveness and gaining more by producing more. We, in education, are in the business of teaching people to think, to create, and to contribute to society as a whole. These are clearly two very distinctly different goals. Should education become reduced to another example of supply and demand? If a student does well on the new universally standardized assessments in high school, does that mean he/she can have a spot in college? Should we segregate based on one test score? Are we doing that now?

Another assumption surrounding business being beneficial to and successful in the field of education is the illusion that occupational fields are interchangeable. Because someone is a secretary in a church, does that mean he/she can step into the role of a private secretary to the CEO of a Fortune 500 company? If someone is a private practice medical doctor in an urban setting does that stand to reason that he/she can be successful in a trauma center at a large metropolitan university hospital? Answers to these questions are debatable although the individual is in the same field. Can a principal in a large rural school district assume to have the ability to run Bill Gate's company? Would Bill Gates let it happen? We, educators, must begin to assert ourselves in making the

## Standards and Standardization

statement that we are the professionals in our field. Teachers are capable of creating curriculum, and we are the experts in presenting that content to our students. Unfortunately, I believe we have done a poor job in standing up for ourselves, and in our silence others have infiltrated our profession attesting to their perceived, over-stated qualifications.

Teach For America (TFA) supports and encourages certified college graduates in any field to enter the professional field of education.[40] TFA is a non-profit company with reported revenue of $270 million in 2011 alone. Interestingly, but not surprising, Bill and Melinda Gates Foundation, the Eli and Edythe Broad Foundation, and the Walton Family Foundation are financial supporters of TFA. One problem is TFA teachers are committed contractually to take the first job offered to them with a two-year commitment to work where they are told to, primarily at charter schools. A high percentage–more than half–of TFA teachers leave their schools immediately after their two-year commitment is completed. This high turnover creates a revolving door effect and is detrimental to the target population, namely charter school children, which they proclaim to serve.[41] I am reminded of the movie *Kindergarten Cop* with Arnold Schwarzenegger as a police officer who is forced to take over a kindergarten classroom, replacing a teacher that had held the position for 25 years. At the end of the movie, he is offered a full-time teaching position because he so readily proved that any occupation could transfer skills to teaching.[42] TFA and even images of teaching in the media continue the blatant devaluing of the teaching profession and make it appear as if being a teacher does not require the development and on-going cultivation of specific knowledge and skills about teaching, learning, and curriculum studies.

40. Kopp, "Teach for America."
41. Ingersoll, "Teacher Shortage," 16–31.
42. Weber and Mitchell, *"That's Funny,"* 95–97.

## ACCOUNTABILITY AND ASSESSMENT

One of many negative effects of government intervention heavily controlling the teaching profession is the overindulgence of testing in our school setting; not to mention the tie of testing to teacher evaluation. It has become detrimental to our professional evaluation to deviate from nationally endorsed standards for fear of negative test results. Coupling scores with teacher evaluation renders a teacher debilitated, forced not only to follow national standards, but to teach the content with little digression from the exact criteria that will be tested. Even if teachers utilize the most efficient instructional methods to presumably increase test scores, there looms a fear of failure if they deviate from the prescribed standards. The increased stress from government intrusion is eroding existing trusting relations and invariably causing a negative impact on the profession.[43] The audit culture that currently exists in education in the U.S., places faculty under surveillance which is "severely constraining judgment, discretion, and professional decision-making"[44] for teachers. Over dependence on high-stakes testing creates "an environment compromised by fear"[45] and we are losing teachers because of the impact of politics and standardization coupling.[46]

All states receiving federal funds must use national standards and evaluate teacher performance based on student performance. Currently in Ohio, Substitute House Bill 362 has adjusted, yet again, the calculation for teacher evaluation. As of publication of this book, 42.5 percent of teacher evaluation is based upon their students meeting value added accountability measures; 42.5 percent is based on teacher performance measures (e.g., observation) and a recently added 15 percent for an alternative component, which consists of four choices but the list of "department-approved components" is not yet released. Value added component

---

43. Conley and Glasman, "Fear, the School Organization," 63–85.
44. Price, "Teacher Education under Audit," 211–225.
45. Ball, "Teacher's Soul and the Terrors," 215–228.
46. Donaldson and Moore Johnson, "FTA Teachers," para. 8.

measures student growth from year to year using standardized test scores. When value-added data is available from the state assessments, it must be used in the student growth measures calculation. If value added information is not available to measure student growth, schools must choose a different assessment that has been provided by national testing vendors and approved by the state. When this data is obtained either from standardized tests or nationally suggested vendor assessments, a student growth measure is calculated. This undisclosed statistical method is then used to measure the impact schools and teachers have on students' academic progress rates from year to year. The remainder 42.5 percent of the evaluation for teachers is based on the teacher performance measure. A principal must evaluate teachers by conducting multiple walkthroughs and two formal observations, including a pre-conference, an observation, post-conference, rubric on-line, and formal written report, which is all to be completed by the start of May each year.[47]

The impact of testing being tied to evaluations is not isolated to Ohio. Educators in participating states across the U.S. are handed national content standards that are assessed by nationalized tests, compared with other classes, communities, states, and nations, with the results tied directly to the evaluation of the teachers and principals. Teachers' livelihoods are directly tied to their ability to disseminate the national standards and the testing capability of all children to represent that information on a timed test. Only 1 percent of special education students are excluded from the results by taking an alternative assessment if they fit very specific criteria. The percentage of students permitted to take the alternative assessment does not come close to the number of special education students. For example, in 2013 the State of Ohio reported 14.8 percent of students identified as having a disability, subtract the 1 percent of those excluded from testing and teachers are being evaluated on all students including the remaining 13.8 percent of students which have proven disabilities.

47. Ohio Department of Education, "Value-Added."

Very alarming is the oversimplification of a very sophisticated occupation of teaching as well as the complex process of learning. Measuring a qualitative occupation, such as the act of teaching, is a difficult task indeed and is not made simple by a formula.[48] How is teacher effectiveness quantified? How is student attitude measured? Individual ability level cross-referenced to test results? We know over-amplification of the importance of testing is not good for education but how did we arrive at this juncture?

Teachers use multiple forms of data to make informed classroom decisions about their content and assess their students. The argument is not about assessing students, the argument is the value and use of standardized tests to base the accountability of schools and the evaluation of teachers. Thomas A. Schwandt does an outstanding job recapping assessment in his book *Evaluation Practice Reconsidered*.[49] He outlines the changes in the teaching profession and how we have evolved from consultants to evaluators that are forced to seek a decision that is evaluative, preoccupied in producing knowledge to be measured. A more humanistic look at role of the teacher is to value human differences through dialogue making people "morally answerable rather than technically accountable for their actions."[50] Schwandt presents a look at practical hermeneutics, which values the importance of interchange that questions subject matter as well as a self-questioning process: wherein "neither the evaluator nor the practitioner is thought to face a problem to be solved as much as a dilemma or mystery that requires interpretation and self-understanding."[51]

Assessment done in this manner can be messy. Misunderstandings are expected, and we risk confusion about others and ourselves as we mutually seek to understand each other and the situation at hand. This leaves room for the professional, i.e., the teacher, to compile the evaluation material and come to a conclusion if the subject matter has been assimilated. No matter the

---

48. Cochran-Smith, "Unforgiving Complexity of Teaching," 3–5.
49. Schwandt, *Evaluation Practice Reconsidered*.
50. Ibid., 23.
51. Ibid., 69.

philosophy of evaluation you favor, the main objective remains clear, we need to be "asking in whose interests should we be acting and to what purpose. These are ethical questions and they should take precedence over technical questions of how to do evaluations."[52]

One major paradigm shift[53] today ties teacher evaluation to student growth thus valuing teacher effectiveness rather than teacher quality.[54] The Standards for Educational Accountability Systems[55] produced by The National Center for Research on Evaluation Standards and Student Testing (CRESST) refer to twenty-two rigorous guidelines for test validity. Strict adherence to all twenty-two guidelines is required to be considered credible. Using Ohio as an example, there are many violations to these guidelines for using test scores for anything other than student achievement. "To be dismissed from a teaching job because of value added scores is to be dismissed for reasons entirely beyond the professional control of that teachers irrespective of the actual quality or effectiveness of the teacher."[56] Hoover argues that the test is not valid and we are continuously allowing standardized evaluations to be conducted without supportive evidence that they actually "prove" intelligence.

James Popham[57] contributes three distinct reasons why standardized tests do not measure teacher effectiveness. Firstly, classroom content does not always match what is being tested. Schools are underfunded; books are outdated and do not match the standards so there is a strong mismatch between what is taught and what is actually tested. Secondly, test questions answered correctly by 80 percent or more of the practice test takers do not make it past the final cut on standardized test development. Simply put, test questions on which students perform well do not make it onto the actual standardized tests that are used. The better job teachers

52. Ibid., 154.
53. Jacobs, *Curriculum 21*.
54. Stumbo and McWlaters, "Measuring Effectiveness," 10.
55. National Center for Research on Evaluation, "Standards," 1–7.
56. Hoover, "Understanding the Basic Problems," 5.
57. Popham, "Why Standardized Tests Don't Measure," 8–15.

do teaching a topic, the less likely the questions will appear on the actual test. Thirdly, not everyone has the same intellectual ability and not all content for the test is a reflection of what is learned in school. What does this mean? Teacher evaluations based on standardized tests negate individual intelligence levels and ignore socioeconomic status. Outside influences idolization of standardized testing is unhealthy and uses data from tests not proven valid.

One study that analyzed 593 schools district Proficiency Test results "confirmed what every experienced teacher knows intuitively, student academic performance is primarily a function of the student's living conditions (family, neighborhood, health, nutrition opportunity) outside school."[58] Achievement on the standardized tests proved to have a direct correlation with socioeconomic status not school achievement, yet we continue to value these tests. The exaggerated dependence on standardized test results has caused multiple negative effects. Some effects include, but are not limited to, teaching to the test, student cheating, control of curriculum from educators to organizations, and harmful levels of stress just to name only a few.[59] So, why do we rely on standardized testing as a level of intellectual intelligence? Do we, as teachers, truly value the information we glean from this one form of evaluation?

Yong Zhao does an excellent job of pointing out the exchange of educational agendas currently taking place between the United States and China. In, *Catching Up or Leading the Way*, Zhao states that there are "two paths in front of us; one in which we destroy our strengths in order to 'catch-up' with others in test scores and one in which we build our own strengths so we can keep the lead in innovation and creativity."[60] Zhao contends that nationalizing standards produces, "a homogenous group of individuals with the same abilities, skills and knowledge. Such a result will be disastrous to America and Americans because globalization and technology continue to change the world; America needs a citizenry of creative individuals with a wide range of talents to sustain its

58. Hoover, "Understanding the Difference," para. 3.
59. Armstrong, *Best School*.
60. Zhao, *Catching Up or Leading the Way*, xii.

tradition of innovation."⁶¹ While China is busy learning about our past philosophy of education, we are mimicking their standardized system. If we look only at the test results, quantitative differences between what we are being told are high performing countries and low performing countries, we lose what really matters, the philosophical, qualitative approach to education and the rich, descriptive details it offers us about our professional work.

## CONCLUSION

We are a country founded on the principal that government is responsible for representing its individual citizens. The government derives their powers from the consent of those governed.⁶² Nancy is clear about democracy being the truest expression of all being together, an expression in which everyone has value in a shared existence and we all take responsibility for our individual selves and for each other.⁶³ Currently, what we are seeing in the United States is power and money in politics, not democracy. Apparently something is prohibiting us in education from taking action to release the strangle-hold that neoliberalism has on our profession. What is stopping us from standing up against standardized management? Why are so many of us just leaving the profession that we once loved⁶⁴ rather than fight to change it?

This chapter exposed information on the standardization of public education and infiltration of government control over curriculum. Chapter 2 will explore the effects this excessively controlling atmosphere has created and its impact on teachers. The chapter goes on to encourage taking back this control.

---

61. Ibid., x.
62. National Archives, "Declaration of Independence."
63. Nancy, *Truth of Democracy*.
64. Kopkowski, "Why They Leave."

# 2

# Freedom from Oppression

"Through manipulation, the dominant elites can lead the people into an unauthentic type of "organization," and can thus avoid the threatening alternative: the true organization of the emerged and emerging people. The latter have only two possibilities as they enter the historical process: either they must organize authentically for their liberation, or they will be manipulated by the elites."[1]

"We achieve freedom through confrontation with and partial surpassing of such weight or determinacy. We seek this freedom, however, only when what presses down (or conditions or limits) is perceived as an obstacle. Where oppression or exploitation or pollution or even pestilence is perceived as natural, as a given, there can be no freedom. Where people cannot name alternatives or imagine a better state of things, they are likely to remain anchored or submerged."[2]

1. Freire, *Teachers as Cultural Workers*, 129.
2. Greene, *Releasing the Imagination*, 52.

## Freedom from Oppression

In order to be free from oppression, there has to be a realization on behalf of individuals that they are, in fact, being oppressed. The beginning of this chapter addresses the internal conflict experienced due to oppression that is seen in the repressed anxiety commonplace today in the field of public education. This overbearing weight causes educated professionals to whisper their feelings of perceived inadequacy to each other in the hallway yet negates the urge to stand against a prescribed curriculum and excessive testing of students. There are those that would question the appropriateness of the term oppression when referring to teaching. The argument could be made that oppression correlates to say issues of wealth, women's rights, or religious believers persecuted for their ideals. The idea of having a "lucrative" career in teaching and being considered oppressed may come under scrutiny. Kincheloe and McLauren support a societal oppression as a class distinction that is "both logically and historically distinct from other forms of exclusion" and that it is "essentially human-made."[3] Within this chapter, I leave the reader to decide if correlations can be made to characteristics of oppression and the teaching profession today. I ask that you sit with the terminology I use and do not exert too much energy on arguing semantics of using the word oppression. Instead, strive to better understand the descriptions and the severity of the circumstance that befalls us as educators.

I begin by defining and describing oppression through the words of Paulo Freire whom I believe was an authority on the subject particularly given his first-hand experiences confronting societal oppression in South America. The second half of the chapter describes democracy in its truest sense alongside liberation from mandated directives applied to the teaching profession. The discussion on democracy and liberation utilizes wisdom of those that dare to speak for freedom.

---

3. Kincheloe and McLaren, "Rethinking Critical Theory," 322.

## OPPRESSION

Freire saw oppressors "using science and technology as unquestionably powerful instruments for their purpose: the maintenance of the oppressive order through manipulation and repression."[4] In order to dominate, the oppressor must deter the drive to search out information, contain curiosity, and thereby restrict the restlessness that comes with creative power. The oppressor must attempt to destroy any illusion the oppressed may have of impacting the world. They "mythicize" the world to reinforce "deceit designed to increase their alienation and passivity."[5] Because the oppressors are often fewer in number, they cannot tolerate unification of the people. In this instance, the oppressed are regarded as "potential enemies who must be watched" enforcing "the necessity for constant control"[6] fueled by isolation, a divide and conquer mentality. Dividing people helps preserve the status quo and allows the dominators to present themselves as saviors of the dehumanized oppressed.

Oppression begins with a false sense of generosity. For the oppressor, money is the primary objective and the goal is profit. The desire of the oppressor is "to have more—always more—even at the cost of the oppressed having less or having nothing."[7] This false generosity releases the guard of the oppressed opening an avenue for vulnerability then acceptance. The oppressor thinks about the oppressed only in a token sense, that is, enough to know them better in order to dominate them more efficiently. There is never total inclusion in decisions but an illusion of participation to gain information. It is essential that the oppressors convince the oppressed that they are being defended against something. An example of this in the case of education is the demise of the U.S. status among other nations in relation to test scores. This residual fear, which has been imposed upon us since Sputnik, allows the

---

4. Freire, *Pedagogy of the Oppressed.*
5. Ibid., 120.
6. Ibid., 41.
7. Ibid., 40.

government to step in to "save" public education. Once this illusion is accepted by the oppressed, the "dominant elites try to conform the masses to their objectives"[8] by creating a false impression of dialogue but the true objectives are determined by the dominate elites. The illusion of teacher created standards when there was only token participation comes to mind.

For the oppressed, there is an illusion of everyone working toward the same goal. In the instance of educational reforms, the goal is for the betterment of our country and our common investment in one of our most valuable resources, future generations of Americans. We followed this illusion created by the dominant forces and unknowingly became instruments in the expectations of standardized management. "The oppressed who have adapted to the structure of domination in which they are immersed, have become resigned to it, are inhibited from waging the struggle for freedom so long as they feel incapable of running the risks it requires."[9]

Such authoritarianism has caused "apathy, excessive obedience, uncritical conformity, lack of resistance against authoritarian discourse, self-abnegation and fear of freedom."[10] Oppression creates a true fear from the departure of rules of the dominant force. There is a fear of risk because not only do the oppressed struggle with separation from the authority but also confrontation from others that remain oppressed. There are those not yet realized, those that conform to standardization, with either outward positive support or complete apathy. Some choose conformity to keep security rather than risk the fear of the unknown. Even when there is a realization that change is necessary, there is an internal struggle with "prescriptions or having choices," "human solidarity or alienation," "being spectators or actors," and in "speaking out or being silent."[11] Though the choice seems morally clear, fear takes hold negating choice. When oppression is perceived as natural or

8. Ibid., 128.
9. Ibid., 29.
10. Freire, *Teachers as Cultural Workers*, 40.
11. Freire, *Pedagogy of the Oppressed*, 30

a given, it will remain intact. "When people cannot name alternatives, imagine a better state of things, share with others a project of change, they are likely to remain anchored or submerged."[12] If people are "afraid of acknowledging structures, they can scarcely think of breaking through them to create others, to transform."[13] In other words, if people cannot name the obstacles, they do not know where the struggle lies. In order to desire freedom, people must first realize they are not free in the present. Until those in education realize that our rights have slowly been removed, we will not have awareness that we are, in fact, oppressed and thus remain neutral.

## NEUTRALITY

The fear is linked to a debilitating incapacity to do anything at all, an indecisiveness that has caused stagnant neutrality. This temporary nullification of teachers voices "must not, in the name of democracy, evade the responsibility of making a decision."[14] Remaining neutral is an immoral act because an individual is covering up one's own choices and voice, and doing this always works in favor of the dominant powers. However, from fear courage can be born, and although it is not easy, what does not seem possible is to do nothing or "too little before the terrible afflictions that affect us."[15] Is it wrong to refuse to accept education the way it is today? What good is there in pushing back, will it change anything? These questions remain unanswered, but there is one given, which is it is unethical to do nothing. "The educator does not have the right to be silent just because he or she has to respect the culture."[16] Our moral obligation is to begin to dialogue about what should be, our duty is to intervene.

12. Greene, *Dialectic of Freedom*, 9.
13. Ibid., 9.
14. Freire, *Teachers as Cultural Workers*, 43.
15. Ibid., 50.
16. Bell, Gaventa, and Peters, *We Make the Road*, 132.

We know how to teach. We know the task is joyous and rigorous, that "it is impossible to teach without the courage to love, without the courage to try a thousand times before giving up."[17] Teachers are endowed with the predisposition to fight for what is right, to be vigilant in the "defense of the need to create conditions conducive to pedagogy in schools."[18] We know what is happening in education is wrong as a result of the oppressive nature of standardization. We may not have the exact answer of a utopian classroom or educational system, but we have the power to visualize the endless possibilities when we are empowered with choice and provide that same atmosphere for our students. "Adult society is powerful,"[19] and we can change society if we so choose. We may have a fear of experiencing new things, of exposing ourselves to mistakes, but it is impossible to change without taking the risk. "In fighting for freedom we discover how freedom is beautiful and difficult to be created but we have to believe that it's possible."[20]

## PRAXIS

In order to break from dependence, there must be a transformation—a praxis. Praxis is defined as "reflection and action upon the world in order to transform it."[21] To achieve praxis, the oppressed must confront reality in a critical manner, while simultaneously acting upon that reality. The oppressors do not welcome transgression from conformity because they "want people to continue in a state of submersion."[22] The charge has to be that transgression is not a violent act of attrition but instead a fight for liberation for all parties that is for both the oppressed and the oppressor. Fundamentally, praxis positions itself as a primary right that people who

17. Ibid., 3.
18. Ibid., 4.
19. Ibid., 184.
20. Ibid., 220.
21. Freire, *Pedagogy of the Oppressed*, 33.
22. Ibid., 34.

are "subjected to domination must fight for their emancipation."[23] This process of humility requires an intense faith in the power to "make and remake, to create and re-create" and the faith in an educator's vocation "to be more fully human (which is not the privilege of an elite but the birthright of all)."[24]

Releasing oppression is sought through praxis. Put another way, praxis involves recognizing a problem exists, committing to a transformation, and taking action. The oppressed must first realize there is indeed a problem; "as long as the oppressed remain unaware of the causes of their condition, they fatalistically accept their exploitation."[25] One day I asked a fellow teacher if she felt oppressed, and she quickly responded, "No, not at all." When I asked her why, she stated, "Because I know that none of this was done to us intentionally." Wanting to engage her in a critical-thinking dialogue, I then shared some facts illustrated in Chapter 1 that the current trends in education are, in fact, very political, intentional, and motivated by money. I decided to re-state the question if she felt oppressed. She did not respond. When people are oppressed they tend to distrust themselves. "It is only when the oppressed find the oppressor out and become involved in the organized struggle for their liberation that they begin to believe in themselves. This discovery cannot be purely intellectual but must involve action, nor can it be to mere activism, but must include serious reflection: only then will it be a praxis."[26]

Only when we realize that our oppressors are dehumanizing us can we see that we are in turn, unintentionally dehumanizing our students. Unwittingly and without malice, we have in turn become the oppressor to our students and only in our taking action toward liberation from the oppressed can we free ourselves and those students we take responsibility for. Praxis is the conduit for transformative action within education.

    23. Ibid., 67.
    24. Ibid., 71.
    25. Ibid., 46.
    26. Ibid., 47.

FREEDOM FROM OPPRESSION

## LEADING THE WAY

According to Freire, there are two types of teaching. The first is a banking concept of education where the teacher fills the student with "a topic completely alien to the existential experience of the students," students are positioned as "containers" or "receptacles" to be "filled" by the teacher.[27] In this concept, the lack of inquiry prohibits praxis as knowledge emerges only through invention and reinvention. Knowledge in the banking concept is a "gift bestowed by those who consider themselves knowledgeable upon those whom they consider to know nothing."[28] Oppression and the banking concept go hand in hand because they transform people into receiving objects that seemingly lack and do not encourage the opportunity for empowerment.

Do we want to allow outside forces protecting their supremacy, to produce a façade of our profession in order to justify their necessity? People who are truly committed to a democratic education must reject the deposit of information and replace it with a "problem posing education."[29] The second concept that Freire discussed rejects depositing and embodies communication and dialogue. This liberating type of education rests in "acts of cognition not transferals of information."[30] Through dialogue between the teachers and the students, disagreements are welcomed and expected. There is no one authority present in the classroom and everyone is on the side of discovery. Problem posing education accepts "neither a well-behaved present nor a predetermined future—roots itself in the dynamic present and becomes revolutionary."[31]

Just as those that dominate do not have the right to impose their views on others, we do not have the moral right to be silent in an oppressive situation. Our duty is to begin to dialogue when something is questionable. Our duty is to begin talking about

27. Ibid., 53.
28. Ibid., 53.
29. Ibid., 60.
30. Ibid., 62.
31. Ibid., 65.

the possibility of a better circumstance. This high-level dialogue cannot exist without critical thinking as well as the time necessary to reach this level of synthesis. Critical thinking promotes a transformation rather than the static mindset that evolves from a deposited education. We need to begin the journey of our praxis and invite others to accompany us on the journey, the path to liberation is not sought for people but with people. Human activity is individual and collective, theory and practice, reflecting and doing. If such movement is cultivated, encouraged, and directed, it can be liberating.

First, there must be liberation, and then comes freedom. Action for liberation in a democratic society is our right and our obligation. As citizens of America, we need to put forth every effort to regain our voices and position as professional educators in charge of our own curriculum agenda. Teachers are those delegated to pass on "the democratic ideas in which alone this country is truly a distinctive nation."[32] Thus, with us lies the responsibility to "prove worthy of our heritage"[33] and to "sustain our true national spirit."[34] Dewey knew such responsibility was serious, and he warned against power passing to the hands of the wealthy, "which has been the curse of every civilization in the past, and which our fathers in their democratic idealism thought this nation was to put an end to."[35] He also warned against the central regulation of education and cautioned that unless we embody the spirit of democracy in schools, it will mean the "development of red tape, a mechanical uniformity and a deadening supervision from above."[36] Although Dewey's cautionary words are from the early part of the 20th century, they sound alarmingly familiar when coupled with our present educational landscape.

We in the field of education have taken our liberties for granted, thinking that democracy will work itself out "as long as

32. Dewey, "Nationalizing Education," 269.
33. Ibid., 341.
34. Ibid., 268.
35. Ibid., 268.
36. Ibid., 269.

## Freedom from Oppression

citizens were reasonably faithful in performing political duties."[37] However, the depth of the present neoliberal crisis in our country and in education "is due in considerable part to the fact that for a long period we acted as if our democracy were something that perpetuated itself automatically."[38] We can no longer accept a "go-as-you-please" type of atmosphere where we have been inclined to "let things drift rather than to think out a central, controlling policy."[39] Those who believe in a better end must forge a new path. In forging this path, we cannot only value the end result but must nurture the path for our individual journeys. Our journeys become opportunities for development with emphasis on the means, not the end. Forging new pathways must evolve "from a living faith in our common human nature and in the power of voluntary action based upon public collective intelligence."[40] Educators not only have the authority but the responsibility to move society forward when a social class is oppressed. Even if that target is taped to our back, we, ultimately affect the future of democracy.

Democracy is a way of life that relies on the faith of human nature. It is a belief in the ability of the human experience "to generate the aims and methods by which further experience will grow."[41] Democracy elicits the "emotions, needs and desires so as to call into being the things that have not existed in the past"[42] at the same time giving us hope for the future. Today, we witness politics driving democracy and to distinguish between the two is imperative. "Democracy is first of all a metaphysics and only afterwards a politics. But the latter is not founded on the former. On the contrary, it is but the condition whereby it is exercised."[43] Politics keeps the door open for democracy and the platform for which it is presented. There is no identifiable authority in democracy but is

37. Freire, "Creative Democracy—The Task Before Us," 341.
38. Ibid., 341.
39. Freire, "Nationalizing Education," 265.
40. Freire, "Democracy is Radical," 339.
41. Dewey, "Creative Democracy: The Task Before Us," 343.
42. Ibid., 343.
43. Nancy, *Truth of Democracy*, 34.

rather a desire, or a will, where what "is expressed and recognized is a true possibility of being all together, all and each one among all."[44] Better yet, the idea of democracy as a metaphysics may be to describe democracy as a spirit embodied by people not an institution. True democracy is intangible. There, of course, is value in the exchangeable goods but also in what is not exchangeable "because it is outside all measurable value."[45] This is incalculable and far exceeds politics.

## FREEDOM

What is freedom? An opening of space, a new look on perspectives of all, "with everything depending on the actions we undertake in the course of our quest, the praxis we learn to devise."[46] Freedom is a beginning, the ability to take an initiative and start a dialogue of investigation. Maxine Greene believes in achieving freedom through collegial dialogue for the "sake of personal fulfillment and the emergence of a democracy dedicated to life and decency."[47] We, as Americans, are endowed with freedoms, whether we act upon these freedoms or fight to secure them does not matter, they remain ours. So many of us grew up with the right for freedom without ever questioning or really knowing what that truly means. Maybe the "givenness"[48] of freedom in our lives is taken for granted or perhaps the risks associated with it feel too great. "We know too that, even given conditions of liberty, many people do not act on their freedom; they do not risk becoming different; they accede; often, they submit."[49] It then follows that if we do not take action, we "accept existing structures as a given."[50] I believe teachers are self-directed and value independence for themselves

44. Ibid., 14.
45. Ibid., 15.
46. Greene, *Dialectic of Freedom*, 5.
47. Ibid., xii.
48. Ibid., 115.
49. Ibid., 117.
50. Ibid., 22.

## Freedom from Oppression

and their students, but when these qualities are threatened, action must be taken to regain the freedom lost. Freedom is achieved and maintained when people come together in "speech and action,"[51] therefore, freedom is associated with both dialogue and action.

Unfortunately, we in education have developed a withdrawal from the afflictions of the present day standardized management where there "ought to be an impassioned and significant dialogue"[52] about the circumstance in which we find ourselves. We need to be provoked to reach beyond the stagnation of standardization where extreme conditions prompt true democratic freedom. Freedom that is democratic honors authenticity in its presentation and is mutually pursued with no pretense. Maybe the quest to stifle the inertia of habit will evolve from our morality. "It may only be when we think of humane and liberating classrooms in which every learner is recognized and sustained in her or his struggle to learn how to learn that we can perceive the insufficiency of bureaucratized, uncaring schools. And it may be only then that we are moved to choose to repair or to renew."[53]

The dominant voices we follow today are those of "officials who assume the objective of worth of certain kinds of knowledge."[54] I think we can agree that schools have the power to bring about social change. If we choose to continue passively following a neoliberal oppressive agenda, however, this change will continually be "linked to national economic concerns or used to mask them"[55] rather than robust democratic freedom. We must begin to reflect upon our own teaching practice as well as look at public education as a whole that includes thinking critically about how our actions or inactions are impacting our children, classrooms, buildings, districts, states, and nation. We need to approach teaching and learning with deep concerns for the prescribed, reactive behavior and responses we are forced to extract from our students. We need

51. Ibid., 27.
52. Ibid., 22.
53. Greene, *Releasing the Imagination*, 5.
54. Ibid., 9.
55. Ibid., 11.

to take a strong look at our own action, or lack thereof, and ultimately consider a quest based on discovery of a better way.

    Looking daily at numbers, comparing statistics, and analyzing data it seems impossible to imagine a way out. "When nothing intervenes to overcome such inertia, it joins with the sense of repetitiveness and uniformity to discourage active learning."[56] It is through active learning and creative conversation with peers as educational stakeholders that we can begin to actualize better ways of being in schools. This actualization "has to begin in the local places, in school rooms"[57] because this is where people know each other and are living with the burdens that directly affect public education. We must find ways to create intentional spaces where people choose to engage in "collective action in order to bring about societal repairs."[58] From there, dialogues can unfold that inform actions to "empower individuals to open themselves to what they are making in common."[59] "Imagination may be a new way of de-centering ourselves, of breaking out of the confinements of privatism and self-regard into a space where we can come face to face with others."[60] But only we can choose, individually, to take part in this offer of democratic freedom. This challenge lies in making an informed decision to "break from anchorage" and insert yourself "into the world with a particular kind of identity and responsibility," while continuously "straining toward what ought to be."[61] The public needs to "hear articulate practitioners ask in public what the purposes of U.S. education really ought to be in these times."[62] This informed action requires teachers to make a sustained change.

56. Ibid., 21.
57. Ibid., 59.
58. Ibid., 66.
59. Ibid., 59.
60. Greene, *Releasing the Imagination*, 31.
61. Ibid., 71.
62. Ibid., 170.

## CONCLUSION

Today, power has replaced political sense. Neoliberal oppression has caused neutral conformity where there ought to be a call for democratic liberation. We need to always remember the definition of democracy, where our individual value is innately our contribution and value for life that "comes only from shared existence."[63] We must begin to imagine, though praxis, taking responsibility for each other to create openings for true democratic freedom. After all, democracy expects periodic social change to be elicited and devoutly sought after in order to support freedom.

What is change? The theory? The practice? Although the theory behind change is complicated, details of this process have been studied in depth. Simplified, as human beings we need a reason to change. To pursue a different venue than the habit that we often inherit and continue to perpetuate, there must be something that prompts us to change. Chapter 3 discusses several theories of change and presents a number of ideas that support sustaining change. The next chapter also discusses the inevitable byproduct of change, which tends to be conflict.

---

63. Ibid., 31.

# 3

# Sustaining Change

"When people choose to be a part of something bigger, to seek freedom and accept the obstacles that come with that choice, they change."[1]

"You have a choice. Mindsets are just beliefs. They're powerful beliefs, but they're just something in your mind, and you can change your mind."[2]

How do we, as humans, change? It is a simple enough question with a complicated answer. There are many theorists that have dedicated their lives to helping us understand this question. The type of change I am referring to is a change in our approach to education, a democratic approach that sparks renewal. Based on the previous chapters, you may now feel empowered with information on who is controlling the direction of curriculum in education today, and you might also be gaining familiarity

1. Greene, *Dialectic of Freedom*, 110.
2. Dweck, *Mindset*, 16.

with the oppressive state in which we as educators find ourselves. Another piece of the puzzle to the renewal of education is change. Professional educators have not had an outstanding track record for sustaining change in curriculum development. In a review of major curriculum changes over decades, Walker and Soltis found that "most reforms since the progressive era have failed to bring the lasting and substantial changes caused by the reformers."[3] They attribute this failure to the difficulty of lasting and sustained change, but on the other hand, they add that "when teachers support reform and find it relevant to their students' needs" that this change "can be one of the most fulfilling experiences in a teaching career."[4] We need to seek a deliberative change in public education that is sustained over time, one that we believe in. But first, we have to change, as individuals that can help in prompting change as a collective unit. This chapter presents theories of change, both past and present, and applies these theories to sustaining individual change. For purposes of this book, I define sustaining change as a transformation within an individual, specifically a shift of consciousness that involves replacing a previous belief or mindset with a new one and replicating it on a daily basis.

### CHANGE THEORY

One well-known theory for change in education is Lewin's Change Theory[5] Schein described Lewin's Change Theory as "the ability to balance the amount of threat produced by discomforting data with enough psychological safety to allow the change target to accept the information, feel the survival anxiety, and become motivated to change."[6] In other words, we must realize the uneasiness of the problem, trust the environment in which change will occur, and gather information for motivated action. Lewin believed that even

---

3. Walker and Soltis, *Curriculum and Aims,* 82.
4. Ibid., 88.
5. Levin, *Resolving Social Conflicts.*
6. Schein, "Kurt Lewin's Change Theory," 5.

when people in a group have many different dispositions, if they share a common objective, they can come together as a group.[7] There are three stages to change in his theory: unfreezing, changing, and refreezing.

In the stage of unfreezing, there must exist dissatisfaction or frustration in or with something. In the case of this book, for example, the frustration many of my colleagues and I have is with the excessive demands of mandated assessments and evaluation methods resulting from the standardized management of public education. During the unfreezing stage, it is necessary to overcome individual resistances and group conformity. Much discussion takes place where all views must be shared and experienced, and people can begin to adopt their own views. Trust is vital within the unfreezing stage for informed dialogue because people are brainstorming ideas and actively participating in acknowledging the problems at hand thereby recognizing the need for change,

In the second stage of changing there must be an inner personal tension in order to prompt change. For example, a moral dilemma those of us in education face is using teaching methods supporting mandated curriculum that are not age appropriate or conducive for our students' democratic development. During this stage there are two assumptions: (1) the intention to reach a goal corresponds to the tension within the person, and (2) the tension is released if the person reaches the goal. Changing takes time so you must be mindful of all aspects of the learning environment (i.e., the platform of professional development supporting the change). The change will not be sustained if the environment is not conducive to learning.

In the final stage, refreezing, behavior is then considered a function of the person and the environment; they are intertwined. If beliefs change and are not supported, behavior may change temporarily but will not be sustained. As beliefs change, so too must the actions of the teacher, and both beliefs and actions must be supported in the work environment. As a teacher changes their beliefs, if they are not supported in the environment where they

---

7. Smith, "Kurt Lewin."

practice, they will either hide their beliefs or resort back to old habits. According to Schein, "it is best to train the entire group that holds the norms that support the old behavior" for refreezing to be entirely successful and completely supported.[8]

While Lewin's Change Theory as described above looks at how people change in targeted groups, Guskey recently called for a more nuanced, refreshed approach of theory about change.[9] Guskey looks for enduring change in teacher attitudes and encourages continued research on change. He believes strongly that current models of change follow the Lewin model and he questions the validity of this for educators. He argues that our perspectives on teacher change evolved largely from models developed by early change theorists who derived many ideas from psychotherapeutic models about affecting change. An alternative model that re-examines the process of teacher change is needed; a model that looks at change in beliefs and practices.

Although much of his work is not in the field of education rather philosophy, it is my opinion that Frank Ryan[10] has met this call. He provides us with his interpretation of a model of change using the work of the great American educational philosopher, John Dewey and his colleague, Arthur F. Bentley. Ryan's work introduces the circuit of inquiry.[11] Ryan begins his book with an explanation of transaction by Charles S. Peirce's in his circle of doubt-belief.[12] Peirce's theory of change begins with a habit that is in place but becomes interrupted by doubt, which initiates inquiry leading to a cognitive solution. John Dewey and Arthur F. Bentley take this philosophy further by adding greater detail, referring to their model as circuit of inquiry.[13] It is through this model we

---

8. Schein, "Kurt Lewin's Change Theory," 11.

9. Guskey, "Staff Development and Teacher Change." Guskey, "Professional Development and Teacher Change."

10. Ryan, *Seeing Together*.

11. Dewey and Bentley, *Knowing and the Known*.

12. Ryan, *Seeing Together*, 21–22.

13. Ibid., 26–31.

as teachers can begin to understand and incorporate sustained change.

Dewey and Bentley's transactional vision of change is one that involves an on-going circuit of inquiry moving from: nonreflection, habit, disruption, problem, hypothesis, experiment, and object. Using this model, it is of the utmost importance that we realize that in order to move from a nonreflective state, we must recognize that there is a problem that cannot be solved by existing habit; that is, a habituated response is not always the right venue for solving the problem. Applying this theory to our current plight, we would have to recognize the over reliance of the standardized management paradigm in education as a problem big enough to move past the inertia of habit. Dewey and Bentley acknowledge that we are comfortable in our nonreflective state. It is in our nature to want to remain comfortable in this state of security. Nonreflection can give us a false sense of being "safe" making it not feel natural for us to break away. Below I elaborate more on each feature in the circuit of inquiry.

Nonreflective Experience—Involves normal classroom practices; routines developed by going through the process of problem-solving previously and are now acted upon without thought, the habit of a nonreflective experience. This is the daily routine that teachers exhibit when lesson plans are in order, class goes smoothly, standards are met for the day, and there are no problems that cannot be solved easily.

Habit—Something causes a disruption in this nonreflective experience and one of two things can happen. Either the habit will prompt the educator to act in a certain way, causing continuation of the nonreflective experience or, and this is key, the disruption will become a problem. A problem that causes anxiety prohibits sustaining the habit. In reference to the ideas in this book, now that we have discovered the problem of neoliberal control and explored the effects of oppression, it is my hope that teachers may believe that this problem is big enough to break out of the cycle of nonreflective experience.

Problem—When there is a problem: (a) diagnose the problem (this may involve a hypothesis, tools, and testing); (b) develop a hypothesis or a plan for resolving the problem; or (c) determine and obtain the data and tools needed for testing the hypothesis. If together we have diagnosed the problems in public education today, we can move on to creating a hypothesis for resolving the problem. Imperative to moving forward in a transactional model of change is creating a hypothesis to solve the problem within an environment that provides support for the last step in problem solving, collect tools needed for testing the newly created hypothesis.

Experiment—Take the hypotheses or tools and data back to the work environment. Using the hypothesis in the classroom provides needed information and data for making adjustments, a perfect example of theory and practice.

Object—The object of the entire process is the satisfactory resolution of the problem, which prompts a return to a new and enriched non-reflectivity. When a solution is achieved, we have succeeded in changing of our belief system and how we function. "Once a solution is achieved, thought has served its purpose and a state of habituated belief is restored. It is not the original belief, however, but belief informed by what we have learned through the function of inquiry."[14] In our case, the teaching practice has changed and the mindset of the educator is different than his/her original thinking, and the practice is sustained through continued support provided in the work environment.

## CHANGE IN MINDSET

One way in which educational professionals can disrupt the "inertia of habit"[15] is to change our minds. We do have that right and choice. But why is changing one's mindset much harder for some than others? Carol S. Dweck believes change is harder for some

14. Ibid, 21–22.
15. Greene, *Releasing the Imagination*, 21.

people rather than others because we humans generally function within one of two mindsets: a fixed mindset and a growth mindset.[16] People with a fixed mindset believe that our innate qualities are "carved in stone."[17] This type of person believes that you must prove yourself constantly, and they value quantitative intelligence while possessing an enormous amount of fear, almost debilitating, of making mistakes. An error, to the person with a fixed mindset, is perceived as less than intelligent so venturing outside the box of security is avoided. On the opposite side, people with a growth mindset value creativity along with new ideas and are at ease brainstorming. Such people value new ideas and usually act upon them. Growth mindset individuals believe that our basic qualities are things that are cultivated through effort. Growth is an ability that is developed by achievement through applied learning. This type of person believes wholeheartedly in the ability of human development, loves to learn, and conceptualizes mistakes as a sign of a work in progress.

If you have an outside force inflicting the urgency of quantifying intelligence, a fixed mindset will be promoted. The standardized management paradigm in the field of education supports, and even creates, a fixed mindset mentality. "The idea that one evaluation can measure you forever is what creates the urgency for those with a fixed mindset."[18] It is not hard to imagine that a large group of people within an environment that has promoted a fixed mindset would not be knocking down the door to break out of such conformity. Even if a fixed mindset is not your natural state of mind, if those around you seemingly follow a fixed mindset, you tend to follow that path. "Who can afford the luxury of trying to grow when everything is on the line right now?"[19] But education should not be fixed.[20] We need to change our mindset, finding way to resist the pretense that the value of individuals, both

16. Dweck, *Mindset*.
17. Ibid., 6.
18. Ibid., 29.
19. Ibid., 20.
20. Gomez, Black, and Allen, "Becoming a Teacher."

children and teachers, is based solely on quantitative measures. In other words, the change we need to seek is one of education for the potential of human development.

Through thirteen years as an administrator, I have worked with enough teachers to know that a large majority of us in this profession have a growth mindset. I believe this is our natural way of thinking, but it is too often quietly hidden in conformity for self-preservation. To me this is a nonreflective state, and our perpetuation of this in practice does not align with our beliefs. If our beliefs are of a growth mindset, then why is our practice not aligned with our beliefs? If the ultimate goal is the renewal of public education, a change in the practice of teachers seems to be the path to conceptualizing such change. But how do we change practice and do our beliefs tie into sustaining that practice? If we presume change in teachers' beliefs are linked to change in their practice, does this ultimately change our educational system? My research and experience support the notion that change in teachers' beliefs promote change in practice. Consequently, changing together to renew education would employ an insurmountable impact on public education today.

## WHAT COMES FIRST, THE CHICKEN OR THE EGG?

Do we change practice because of our beliefs or vice versa? When I conducted a pilot study on a professional development model,[21] I quickly came to the realization that although beliefs may be verbalized, when you see teachers in action, their verbalized beliefs and actions of practice do not always align. In my study, there was a noticeable disparity between what the teachers said in the interview (i.e., their beliefs) from what took place in the classroom observation (i.e., their practices). In my experience, if beliefs and practices are not aligned, the change in practice is short-term. Accordingly, change in practice is temporary if not supported by change in beliefs.

---

21. Carothers, "Qualitative Mini-study."

I conducted professional development for many years, and I began to notice a pattern of short-term change in practice that was directly tied to and evaluated by standardized measurement. The frustration of this limited, short-term change in practice prompted me to begin a quest to find the key characteristics of what constitutes sustaining adult change. Low scores on the standardized Ohio Achievement Tests in short-answer and extended-response items prompted an initiative in professional development entitled, "Writing about Math." The focus began with math teachers in the fifth and sixth grades, and over the next year, the initiative grew to include all math and language arts teachers from the fifth through eighth grades. At the time, I was in a doctoral program so it was an easy fit for me in my position to research theory in professional development and to set the stage for the initiative. The results over the next two years were staggering, and the initiative was considered a success; practice was assumed to have changed which in turn raised test scores.[22]

*Middle School Math Results Gr. 6 Short Answer/Extended Response Averages*

|  | 2004 | 2005 |
|---|---|---|
| Questions Above State Average | 3 | 6 |
| Questions At State Average | 1 | 3 |
| Questions Below State Average | 8 | 3 |

Unfortunately, four years after this professional development initiative, the middle school results on short-answer and extended-response questions resorted back to below the state average. This turn of events prompted our district to distribute a short narrative survey to teachers to ascertain topics that could be addressed in future professional development initiatives. Surprisingly, the teachers responded by stating that there was a need for professional development in extended-response and short-answer questions on math achievement tests, that this topic had not been addressed

22. Samford, "Exploring Sustained Change in Teachers' Beliefs."

in the past. Not only was the change in practice reversed, it was forgotten all together. Why had change not been sustained?

I have come to realize that if only practice changes without a change in teachers' beliefs, that the change seen in practice will not be sustained. The change will be short-term, and when the external force is removed, the teaching practice will return back to its original state. Fullan[23] questions the order and believes a change in practice brings about an alteration of beliefs. The argument between beliefs and practice could be batted around endlessly, but when the dust settles, one thing is clear; both belief and practice must be elicited to achieve a sustained change. Edwards and Hensien[24] conclude, and I agree, change in teacher beliefs is tied into teaching and learning and will ultimately be tied into classroom practice.

In order for there to be sustained change in beliefs, there must be a deep understanding of what change you want and how that change will endure.[25] The idea of sustained change in adult beliefs is fully explored in the work of Robert Kegan. In his first book, *The Evolving Self*, Kegan[26] found alignment to his theory and the work of Piaget (1896–1980), who believed people grow into our world by "a process of adaptation shaped by the tension between the assimilation of new experience to the old 'grammar' and the accommodation of the old grammar to the new experience."[27] Kegan detailed how we organize ourselves as the organism to the world; we are always at issue to find a truce or a new balance. The struggle to find this balance is ongoing throughout our lives and, to some extent, involves a "killing off of the old self"[28] when the we evolve. This growth is very costly and frightening as it involves leaving behind a piece of our old self and evolving into a new place of knowing.

23. Fullan, *New Meaning of Educational Change*.
24. Edwards and Hensien, "Changing Instructional Practice."
25. Guskey, "Professional Development and Teacher Change."
26. Kegan, *Evolving Self*.
27. Ibid., 43–44.
28. Ibid., 232.

In his second book,[29] the above stated theory is interwoven into the demands of the present day, with the constant pressure to change our skill set without the time that is necessary to do so. What is needed to allow for the gradual transformation of the mind is a "blend of support and challenge."[30] Supporting a sustained change requires trust and time. "If a program can fail to provide the necessary evolutionary support by neglecting to build a bridge out of and beyond the old world, it can also fail by expecting its charges to take up immediate residence in the new world."[31] In a third book, Kegan and Laskow-Lahey[32] stated that we must change the way we think and feel; we must change our mindset. In adult learning, we must change our mindset and behavior rather than changing only behavior because "neither change in mindset or change in behavior alone leads to transformation, but that each must be employed to bring about the other."[33] Therefore, sustained change is a transformative change in one's mindset that is accepted and replicated on a regular basis. The person knows when he/she has changed his/her belief system and he/she is a different person, on a different level, because of this change.

## APPLIED LEANING THEORY

Our brains are made for growth. James Zull[34] applies biochemistry to the learning cycle and offers positive information. Our brains do, in fact, change! There is a reaction when we learn that creates an actual physical change in our brain. The relation between the structure of our brain and learning is illustrated by four main parts of our brain. Over-simplified, the brain is broken into sections: the sensory (i.e., how we sense signals from the outside world), the

29. Kegan, *In Over Our Heads.*
30. Ibid., 42.
31. Ibid., 46.
32. Kegan and Laskow-Lahey, *Immunity to Change.*
33. Ibid., 309.
34. Zull, *Art of Changing the Brain.*

back and the front integrative cortex (i.e., where signals are pulled together and recognized in the sum of all information), and the motor (i.e., movement into action). Applying physical brain function to an uncomplicated cycle of learning, Zull relies on ideas he compiled from Dewey and Piaget. Most importantly from Zull's work, we can conclude that we are in charge of our own learning. If we decide not to change (e.g., fear of failure inhibits us from taking action), we do not complete the learning cycle therefore remaining unchanged. As one experienced teacher I know added, "Personally, I think this is why so many of us don't change, because of the fear of failure." There is a part of our brain for receiving information and integrating that information to our past knowledge. There is also a second part for acting upon and modifying that information, and "if we are to learn in the way that transforms, we must use both of these parts of the brain."[35] Meaning, we must process new information and act upon it or sustained learning does not take place.

However, both positive and negative emotions have direct effect over our ability to complete the learning cycle. Detecting emotions are the first impulse when new information is received. Fear or pleasure can stop growth or inhibit change. If we are afraid that we will be harmed either physically or mentally, our brain is instantly aware of our feelings and immediately overpowers cognition. An awareness about our emotions can have a remarkable impression upon our ability to change. The pursuit of positive input or the avoidance of negative input impacts whether we complete the growth process. Because so many of us within education are stifled into accepting an unnatural fixed mindset in the culture of standardized management, it is extremely difficult for us to grow or act upon any knowledge we may have either newly obtained or previously held. We are stuck.

---

35. Ibid., 34.

## CHALLENGE OF CHANGE

Change is a challenge. In order to change and to move past habit, there must be a problem that causes enough anxiety that cannot be solved with habit. Whenever the words "anxiety" or "problem" are used, expect that conflict will be mentioned shortly thereafter. Conflict is the unsettling discomfort that is inevitable when many educated people gather to brainstorm higher-level thinking goals. Jim Collins[36] looked at organizational conflict and had this to say from his research; "All the good-to-great companies had a penchant for intense dialogue. Phrases like 'loud debate,' 'heated discussions,' and 'healthy conflict' peppered the articles and interview transcripts from all the companies. They didn't use discussion as a sham process to let people 'have their say' so that they could 'buy in' to a predetermined decision. The process was more like a heated scientific debate, with people engaged in a search for the best answers."[37]

Although I hesitate to use any comparisons from business to education, Collins offers important information on the vast contribution of successful management strategies that may be valuable for our own purposes of renewal. Buckingham and Coffman[38] agree that top leaders support and encourage colleagues to change through mutual resolution. They change together working through conflict as it inevitably occurs. Kegan[39] acknowledged that when conflict occurs the focus should not be on solving the problem. Instead, focus should be on ways to let the conflict transform the participants as they discover together a mutual resolution to the problem. Conflict should be expected, embraced, and looked at as an opportunity for discussion and discovery.[40] In other words, we should value the creative tension that is inevitable with human

36. Collins, *Good to Great*.
37. Ibid., 77.
38. Buckingham and Coffman, *First, Break all the Rules*.
39. Kegan, *In Over Our Heads*.
40. Feiman-Nemser, "From Preparation to Practice." 1013–1055.

interaction.[41] We may never achieve consensus, but at the very least we will expand democratically beyond individual opinions and grow together with new ideas.

Unfortunately, this way of addressing change is not present within the current system of education. Our system avoids conflict and values conformity. We tend to take a position and avoid the negotiation of a heated discussion for fear of conflict. Ignoring negotiations prompts egos to become involved and promotes positional bargaining. The one who wins a heated discussion becomes the prominent factor. I am reminded of an example of avoiding conflict that I participated in involving a disagreement in services for a student. A representative from our central office and I met with our attorney for several hours before entering a room with the opposing party. The lawyers on both sides spoke for no more than two minutes, and it was decided that we separate to expedite matters and avoid any conflict. For the next three hours, we were in separate rooms with an intermediary running between rooms offering what each party was willing to concede. As you can guess, this process ended with no resolution and there was no growth or change that was brought about as a result.

Growth is filled with conflict and tension, questioning and doubting, changing and growing; we need to have effective strategies in place for conflict resolution.[42] Roger Fisher, William Ury, and Bruce Patton[43] break the act of negotiation away from conflict into two levels: 1) the substance of the issue and 2) the procedure for dealing with the issue. As seen from the negation example above, the substance of the issue was never able to be appropriately addressed because the procedure for dealing with the issue was so restricted. If you provide a platform for working on solving the problem, you are more likely to achieve success. Principled negotiation separates the people from the problem. People work side

---

41. Henderson, "Curriculum Discourse and the Question of Empowerment," 204–209.

42. Clement and Vandenberghe, "Teachers' Professional Development," 81–101.

43. Fisher, Ury, and Patton, *Getting to Yes*.

by side to solve the problem with concentration on the interests of the people. Brainstorming solutions and insisting on using objective criteria lends itself to a more productive negotiation. Just as important as solving the problem is the manner in which you do so. If you want to influence someone, you must "understand empathetically the power of their point of view and to feel the emotional force with which they believe in it."[44] Active listening will reduce the conflict and maximize the initiation of a more constructive dialogue. Solving the problem becomes more about collective interests than taking positions.

Peter Elbow[45] encourages contraries, conflicts, or contradictions. Real learning commences from many points of view. We have to possess the ability to apply already learned concepts to data and to construct new concepts from that data. This requires interaction between people as we "successively climb upon the shoulders of others restructuring so at each climbing up, we can see a little farther."[46] I am sure we have all been in a situation where we felt slighted in a group and hesitated to contribute. The last time I felt this way, which was rather recently, was during a Saturday gathering of several co-authors on a book project. The editor of the book, who I trusted, had an overabundance of editing work to be done, and so I was asked to work on editing my chapter with an associate of his. Most unfortunately, there were several people ahead of me to meet with the associate, time passed, and I was the last of many people to meet with him. The room was starting to clear out, people were leaving and yet multiple comments were made quickly as to the revisions I needed to make in grammar and content. The overwhelming message that I heard was, "I can't believe you are part of this team, and you have a great deal of work ahead of you." I departed abruptly and with very short, curt excuses for my departure. This proud, little Italian woman left thinking, "Who does he think he is?" My stubborn pride mixed with the associates quick comments prohibited me from opening my

44. Ibid., 25.
45. Elbow, *Embracing Contraries*.
46. Ibid., 41.

## Sustaining Change

mind to any suggestions that this professional had added, negating the opportunity for different insight to my original writing. "When people are stubborn and narrow minded, they refuse to allow the material in their head to be restructured by what the other person says. They simply hang on to the orientations they may have and are too afraid to relinquish any of them."[47]

The day after this meeting, the editor called and gave me background on the associate he had chosen for me to work alongside. He talked about his experiences both personally and professionally with this associate and how very qualified he was to help me on my portion of the book. Also, the editor spoke of how he trusted this associate's opinion. Later that day, I had a lengthy conversation with the associate, and he apologized for the manner in which his critique was presented. I too apologized for my closed mindedness of his initial suggestions. I had to trust that he was not going to mentally harm me before I could move on to combine our creative thinking. I soon opened my mind to his interesting and valuable opinions. I had to trust that our combined creative thoughts would surpass my singular previous knowledge. If we let our ideas interact, they can produce ideas or resonate various points of view that we may not have produced had we worked alone. The wisdom that could flow from great, open discussions about curriculum and teaching with intelligent professionals that know their field could produce the motivation for educational renewal. As Zull's research clearly stated "motivation comes from learning."[48] If people are learning and growing, they will be motivated to continue to grow and change will be inevitable–a transformative change that is sustained supporting a renewal of public education.

## CONCLUSION

With the goal of a sustained transformative change from a previous belief or mindset with one that is accepted and is replicated

---

47. Ibid, 41.
48. Zull, *Art of Changing the Brain*, 238.

on a regular basis, we must expect conflict during this process. In this book, we are discussing the problems educational professionals face in public schools. We are acknowledging and exploring the oppressive situations in which teachers find themselves. From this chapter, we have added to these thoughts a model of change that involves the creation of a hypothesis to solve the problem of over standardization of our curriculum. Can we visualize a time where all teachers take responsibility for curriculum development in their building, all on the cutting edge of information, improving professional knowledge as a group? Lorna Earl writes, "It is increasingly clear that deep and productive professional learning is critical to educational change."[49] Now if we realize there is a problem and that we can change our mindsets, next we explore creating the hypothesis for a new way of curriculum development.

---

49. Earl, "Accountability as a Collective Professional Responsibility," 103.

# 4

# The Vastness of Curriculum Development

"What do schools teach, what should they teach,
and who should decide?
Is the primary aim of education to instill basic skills
or foster critical thinking?
Should education aim to mold future citizens, transmit national values,
engender personal development or inspire academic achievement?
Must education have an aim?
And what beliefs, values or attitudes are learned
from the way classrooms are?
That is, what lessons are taught but not planned,
acquired but taken for granted?"[1]

Curriculum is not an easy concept to grasp. As illustrated in the Flinders and Thornton quote above, answers about curriculum usually involve more questions. To make matters worse, there does not seem to be any one perfect answer to "the best"

1. Flinders and Thornton, *Curriculum Studies Reader*, xi.

curriculum method. As we seek school renewal that focuses on inquiry to prompt the needed change in education, we must look ahead to a time when this change will come, and when it does, who should develop curriculum? How do we, the professionals in our field, argue for what is just in educating children if we are not confident enough to articulate what that means? It is our responsibility, those who chose to be in the field of education, to seek answers to the questions of curriculum through critical conversations with our colleagues.

Through the tangled past and into the present, developing curriculum necessitates the guidance of passionate professionals that stand together in the assurance that we are indeed up to the challenge. I encourage you to look at this chapter from a professional growth perspective as a guide through the many theories of curriculum. Better yet, as a timeline through our history ending with a viable alternative to the standardized management paradigm of today. This chapter is filled with theories, both past and present, which may be tedious to some, but is necessary in order to offer a plethora of choice to combine the best pieces from theories for present day practice.

Curriculum development is a messy challenge. Educators and curriculum scholars have tried to organize curriculum in the past but to date the best we have to offer is the present day agenda that boxes our kids into predetermined packages that may be detrimental to their growth as independent, creative, and confident democratic citizens. This chapter offers many diverse theories in order to prompt critical inquiry of an eclectic combination of multiple theories with the goal of practical use in the classroom. I challenge you to delve into this chapter with an open mind for developing curriculum. I propose we review the past in order to support our future in a democratic form of curriculum development that values collegial dialogue and expects change.

THE VASTNESS OF CURRICULUM DEVELOPMENT

## A WALK THROUGH TIME

I begin with Wesley Null's general overview of curriculum development. In his book, *Curriculum: From Theory to Practice*, Null walks through the origin of a liberal curriculum. Liberal curriculum at its heart involves liberal education in the sense of free-minded individuals thinking independently who "have learned to base their judgments on reason and thereby avoid surrendering to their passions, following the directives of other's, or merely pursuing material wealth."[2] Keep in mind, we have not achieved this form of education, but understanding the background of the past compounded with the needs of the present, it seems appropriate to inquire more about this worthwhile idea. As we walk through the past curriculum theories, recognize the mistakes that are seemingly revisited in the present.

Western history takes us back to the Ancient Greek philosopher, Plato who believed that education is empowering, moralistic, and centered on developing the innate potential of the individual. Although liberal in its curricular make-up, Plato thought that the ability to reach this plateau of understanding was not possessed by the masses but by a select few; to educate all people in this manner was thought to be a waste of time. Therefore, those few were placed in positions of power and upon them was bestowed the power of deliberation. Aristotle, too, believed in the rule of communities by elites where "some citizens are responsible for deliberating and making decisions on behalf of the community, while others are responsible for following the decisions made by the elites."[3] This mentality evolved with the emergence of the Christian era. A new message of quality entered with the virtue of "Christ died for everyone."[4] Although faith-based in content, the broader sense of education for everyone began to come into play with a kinder, gentler subject content of hope and acceptance of all. Over time this laid the groundwork for democracy. Public schools began to

2. Null, *Curriculum*, 16.
3. Ibid., 19.
4. Ibid.

dominate and curriculum questions appeared on the scene from liberal arts to economics.

This condensed, general overview of history leads Null into his discussions of five traditions of curriculum in which he applies Joseph J. Schwab's—an important curriculum scholar—work on five education commonplaces (i.e., subject matter, learners, context, teachers, and curriculum making) to illustrate each one. Although not exclusive, the five traditions of curriculum help us see clearly where past curriculum paths traveled and where we are today. None of these perspectives are wrong as there is value is each tradition. You may feel that you "side" or "agree" with one more than another, but each has its place in history and possible value in our future. We begin with a perspective of curriculum that should be familiar to us, systematic curriculum, and move on to existential curriculum, radical curriculum, pragmatic curriculum. and deliberative curriculum.

Systematic curriculum utilizes scientifically-based evidence to support a systems-based form of education; central to this form of curriculum is efficiency and categorization. The emphasis is on effective use of time and measurement of efficiency. It is easy to see similarities in this curriculum perspective in use today. On the contrary, an existential curriculum views education as a personal journey. Individuality and personal meaning would be the focus and choice is imperative in this perspective. Maxine Greene's[5] views as an educator, artist, and activist are a good example of existentialism. Radical curriculum promotes service to society with a distinct want to impact the world. The goal is "equality in mind at all times."[6] The word "radical" comes into play with the example of "critical of anything that resembles a conservative political position."[7] Writing done by the curriculum scholar Michael Apple[8] might serve as a good illustration of radical curriculum work. Pragmatic curriculum is a solution-oriented philosophy

5. Greene, *Dialectic of Freedom, Releasing the Imagination.*
6. Null, *Curriculum,* 87.
7. Ibid., 90.
8. Apple, *Ideology and Curriculum.*

focused on meeting immediate needs. A pragmatic perspective would "avoid definite answers, allowing solutions to remain workable regardless of how circumstances change."[9] Pragmatists want people to solve problems. Lastly, a deliberative curriculum is similar to the law centering on choice and hearing arguments from all sides before seeking a "creative solution to a practical problem."[10] Thus, following a deliberative curriculum "means using our reasoning abilities to imagine alternatives that will move a state of affairs in the direction we want it to go."[11]

Through all of the years of curriculum development, no one theory has left a lasting imprint on our curriculum.[12] I believe this is because there is no one theory, no one quick fix to teaching and learning. Joseph J. Schwab[13] brings to our attention the value of using a montage of theories to support an eclectic type of discipline. He recognizes the usefulness of diversifying relevant to the problems as they present themselves. The eclectic approach to curriculum "recognizes the usefulness of theory to curriculum decisions, takes account of certain weaknesses of theory as ground for decisions, and provides some degree of repair for these weaknesses."[14] The practical use of an eclectic discipline leads to "defensible decisions"[15] whereas methods of theory lead to "warranted conclusions."[16] "No curriculum grounded in but one of these subjects can possibly be adequate, defensible."[17] The use of a theoretic discipline in our curriculum history has not benefited the field of education. A defensible plan must take individuals and society into account along with knowledge, problem solving, and more. To focus on one theory but to ignore another is to lose

9. Ibid., 117.
10. Null, *Curriculum*, 151.
11. Ibid., 168.
12. Walker and Soltis, *Curriculum and Aims*.
13. Schwab, *Science, Curriculum, and Liberal Education*.
14. Ibid., 295.
15. Schwab, "The Practical," 103.
16. Ibid., 103.
17. Ibid., 108.

focus of a whole picture. When we look at various curriculum theories with an eclectic approach, there is more of an encompassing of complexity with respect for change. Through respect for difference, we create dialogue for change that moves us forward together. "We must wrestle the best we can with numerous, largely unconnected separate theories to move from theory to practicality with contributions from all curriculum ideas."[18]

I share the following collection of theorists' ideas to support the use of an eclectic type of curriculum development, one that utilizes a democratic form of inquiry that values collegial dialogue and expects change. John Dewey fought so hard against accepting an either/or mentality in education. "For in spite of itself any movement that thinks and acts in terms of an 'ism becomes so involved in reaction against other 'isms that it is unwittingly controlled by them."[19] Let us not be controlled by one or another theory but take the best of what works in theory and incorporate that into our practice.

## CURRICULUM THEORIES

Teaching from a curriculum theory perspective elicits social emancipation, through complicated conversations[20] that transform the present, not in predictable ways, but "certainly not according to politicians' self-interest agendas."[21] Teaching through the perspective of a curriculum theory approach "seeks the truth of the present state of affairs not the manipulation of them for political purposes, in the present instance, higher test scores on standardized exams."[22] It is my hope that we become comfortable with complicating our conversations, to come together for the purpose of subject, self, and social challenges. I encourage

18. Ibid., 109.
19. Dewey, *Experience and Education*, 36.
20. Pinar, Reynolds, Slattery and Taubman, *Understanding Curriculum*.
21. Pinar, *What is Curriculum Theory*, 207.
22. Ibid., 208.

teachers to follow Pinar's call to "reconstruct themselves through academic knowledge."[23] Do not fear the unknown of curriculum theory presented as conversation. One thing is known, complicated conversation is transformative, the "change is not necessarily predictable, but it is inevitable"[24] and certainly necessary.

I use Flinders and Thornton's book, *The Curriculum Studies Reader*[25] as a guide to present multiple theories in the hope that several may resonate in providing curriculum ideas for today. Using the past as a basis of what to do, or not to do, I support combining the best of curriculum theory for the future. I begin with Franklin Bobbitt. His overwhelming belief in the management of students' interests supported the use of methods of the manufacturing industry and applying them to school curriculum. He thought the methods used to manage industries and their workforce should be applied to education which would bring the same "world-class standards to school curriculum."[26] John Dewey in his published work, "My Pedagogic Creed"[27] refuted a mechanical direction of curriculum with his opinion that education had to begin with insight "into the child's capacities, interests, and habits."[28] Simply put, Dewey valued the power of discovery and thought to repress interest was to weaken curiosity that ultimately deadened interest. He proposed that it was the duty of a community to educate its citizenry and referred to this responsibility as "its paramount moral duty."[29]

Writing about the influence that Bobbitt had over the field of curriculum, Herbert M. Kliebard noted how Bobbitt's influence touted scientific management as the tool for managing schools and this could only be done by curriculum specialists. Even the terminology that Bobbitt coined, "curriculum specialists" implied

23. Ibid., 21.
24. Ibid., 206.
25. Flinders and Thornton, *Curriculum Studies Reader*.
26. Bobbitt, "Scientific Method in Curriculum," 2.
27. Dewey, "My Pedagogic Creed," 17–23.
28. Ibid., 18.
29. Ibid., 23.

a particular set of technical skills unavailable to the untrained.[30] Kliebard disagreed and disapproved of the fallacy in the scientific curriculum movement. Almost sixty-years later, Kliebard noted that there has not been much change; curriculum is still reduced to operations. There is a "failure to recognize the complexity of the phenomena with which we deal" which he felt was "unforgivable."[31] Half a century after Bobbitt's support of industrial influence, little gain has been made in the sophistication of curriculum development.

Ralph Tyler—who built upon Bobbitt's curriculum and teaching thoughts—made history in his book, *Basic Principles of Curriculum and Instruction*[32] using four principles to guide curriculum development: mission, objectives, how to organize the objectives and ultimately, evaluation. In his definition of the intent of this rationale, Tyler was explicit saying "it is not a manual for curriculum construction" and it does not "provide comprehensive guidance."[33] Tyler encouraged colleagues to examine other ideas and develop alternative relationships in effective curriculum. In fact, Tyler wrote in support of Dewey's beliefs that the learner's experience should guide the organizing principals. "It is necessary to note that the criteria, continuity, sequence, and integration apply to these experiences of the learner and not to the way in which these matters may be viewed by someone already in command of the elements to be learned."[34] However, over time, Tyler's rationale was taken-up and became a linear, step-by-step map for curriculum and teacher decisions. It seems we did not follow his philosophy, only simply borrowed his format.

Jumping forward a little in time, Elliot Eisner questioned and brought out the limitations to using objectives in curriculum development. He refuted the scientific approach to curriculum development because of its desires to "identify needed skills, divide

---

30. Kliebard, "Rise of Scientific Curriculum," 38.
31. Ibid., 45.
32. Tyler, *Basic Principles of Curriculum*.
33. Ibid., 51.
34. Ibid., 96.

these skills into specific units, organize these units into experiences and provide those experiences to children."[35] Eisner was a proponent of the rewards of the journey "the joy of the ride, not simply arriving at the destination."[36] He warned that if we value only test scores, that value leaves after the tests are taken and "the only way to have a bull market in schooling is to turn students on to the satisfactions of inquiry in the fields into which they are initiated."[37] Michael W. Apple follows this sentiment, in 2004, lending his voice to the hidden curriculum by recognizing the fact that schools serve "certain social classes rather well and other classes not well at all."[38] His book exposes political control over curriculum, which contributes to inequities of the population. We evaluate a system by "how closely the output of the system satisfied the purpose for which it exists"[39] but who is deciding what the system is; in other words, "the basis for the system itself remains unquestioned."[40] The hidden curriculum resides and lives on when we remain uncritical and do not question why we do the things we do in our educational institutions.

Of deep importance to inquiry around curriculum development is to begin to include discussions over curriculum traditions and to place our attention on the primary task, that is, the purposeful focus for the development of curriculum while making connections between theory and practice. In past curriculum development, we failed to "analyze the [whole] problem closely enough to suggest approaches to its solution."[41] So many past school reform initiatives fail to "connect the criteria of success with theory underlying educational efforts."[42] In other words, we have not done our due diligence in making the connections between

35. Eisner, "Educational Objectives," 86.
36. Eisner, *Kind of Schools We Need*, 42.
37. Ibid.,42.
38. Apple, *Ideology and Curriculum*, 27.
39. Ibid., 105.
40. Ibid., 105.
41. Foshay, "Scientific Inquiry," 93.
42. Short, *Forms of Curriculum Inquiry*, 95.

theory and successful practices. As we educators lead the renewal of our schools, it is time to re-think what we know about and how we understand curriculum development.

## CURRICULUM

At this point, it is appropriate to distinguish a line between education and curriculum. Especially today where it seems as though there is a great deal of discussion over topics of education such as the *Core Content State Standards*, homework with no text books, standardized content, and teacher evaluation. "Much of what passes for talk about education today is shallow and devoid of meaning, if not deceptive."[43] As my stepson so simply and astutely stated, "I can't wait to get done with the tests so we can learn the right way again."

Currently, a growing number of parents and teachers are questioning standards and evaluation of those standards. However, I believe simultaneously that more of us in the field of education need to inquire and push for deliberation about curriculum, not standards but curriculum. If teachers are not seeing, interpreting, and questioning curriculum, it is perceived by those outside of the field as acceptance. Complacency looks like acceptance, but empowerment begins by talking, reading, and questioning the status quo. If by chance the tests were ruled unconstitutional tomorrow, would we be ready? Would the *Core Content Standards* then be thrown out as well? Do we know enough about curriculum development to take on that task ourselves? Our goal for taking back local control of public education is then two-fold. First, teachers must form a unified front against the over importance of the standardized management paradigm, and second, we must be ready to develop curriculum when that force succeeds.

"Curriculum is about what should be taught,"[44] which includes thoughts, and actions, and purpose. Curriculum lends itself

---

43. Null, *Curriculum*, 2.
44. Ibid., 2.

# The Vastness of Curriculum Development

to discussions of "Why do we teach this subject?," "Is it relevant?," and "What is the purpose of this content?" Curriculum forces us to talk and to think about ethics and morals, whereas educational content is commonly discussed without consistently considering right or wrong. As professionals with vested interest in educational renewal, we must recognize when "rhetoric about education is masking the underlying curricular issues that are the essence of education."[45] Foundational curriculum questions about what to teach, how to teach what subject and to whom, how long to teach this content, and what is the overall purpose at its conclusion are answered through dialogue and inquiry. William Schubert eloquently shares his interpretation of the word curriculum.

> One of the most recent positions to emerge on the curriculum horizon is to emphasize the verb form of curriculum, namely, *currere*. Instead of taking its interpretation from the race course etymology of curriculum, *currere* refers to the running of the race and emphasizes the individual's own capacity to reconceptualize his or her autobiography. The individual seeks meaning amid the swirl of present events, moves historically into his or her own past to recover and reconstitute origins, and imagines and creates possible directions of his or her own future. Based on the sharing of autobiographical accounts with others who strive for similar understanding, the curriculum becomes a reconceiving of one's perspective on life. It becomes a social process whereby individuals come to greater understanding of themselves, others, and the world through mutual reconceptualization. The curriculum is the interpretation of the lived experiences.[46]

Curriculum is not stagnant; it changes as we change! As we reflect and grow so do our ideals and therefore our curricula directions. The theory of curriculum as complicated, eclectic conversation negates the present day organization of knowledge, one that is out of context, predetermined, and federally mandated. Curriculum should be more of a guided conversation with a purpose that is

45. Ibid., 4.
46. Schubert, "Reconceptualization of Curriculum," 56.

negotiated and evolves as the conversation grows and from reflection that sparks action. True dialogue sparks reaction and more dialogue.

Over the course of writing this book, I have sought the guidance of a dedicated group of teachers. I meet with them monthly; we call ourselves "The Book Club." Every month as I finish a chapter I mail it to my dedicated "Book Club" members, and they then take time from their lives to read and critique my chapters. After reading chapter 2 on oppression, there was a heated discussion on the implication that teachers were unknowingly oppressing their students. This seemed hurtful to one teacher in particular who refuted the implication by stating that she did not teach in the dictated manner when she closed her classroom door. Ultimately, we decided those teachers fighting the fight behind a cloak of perceived submission exist but what about the students that are in the next classroom? Do they not deserve better? Can teachers truly deviate from the content without punitive damage to their students' test scores? The conversation grew very tense as we challenged each other to think beyond the words and apply the questions to personal classroom experiences. It was then that our book club moved past simply critiquing a book to internalizing a problem.

Today, curriculum has been undermined; it has been reduced to answering other people's questions. We teachers should seek intelligence that is not pre-ordained and look at curriculum as an inquiry into human experience. To teach from a curriculum theory perspective encompasses value for society and self. This enables students to "employ academic knowledge," while they seek to "understand their own self-formation within society and the world."[47] Look at curriculum theory as a quest to "consider your position as engaged with yourself and your students and colleagues in construction of a public sphere, a public sphere not yet born."[48] From this view, our classrooms become a room not yet created but intentionally set up to be a democratic platform for limitless intellectual

---

47. Pinar, *What is Curriculum Theory*, 16.
48. Ibid., 38.

discoveries. Teachers have the right, and obligation, to choose the relations among academic knowledge, the state of society, and the process by which students assimilate the understanding. Brave rebels, who close their doors to teach with their best attempt at restructuring the core standards, struggle professionally and personally with moral obligations. A viable curriculum alternative to today's interpretation of Tyler's 1949 rationale is the curriculum wisdom paradigm[49]

## CURRICULUM WISDOM PARADIGM

According to Henderson and Gornik, there are three paradigms that encapsulate our educational environment: standardized management, constructivist best practice, and curriculum wisdom. Standardized management has a quantifiable place in education without completely focusing on the problem of standardized test scores. Constructivist best practice is linked to a performance of understanding in academic subject area and/or vocational disciplines. Curriculum wisdom is focused on democracy as a moral way of living that incorporates a 3S understanding and includes healthy pieces of each paradigm. Henderson and Gornik challenge educators to advance a problem-solving approach that integrates subject understandings that are integrated with democratic self and social understanding, summarized as a 3S curriculum design. A main focus of the 3S curriculum design is to support both teachers and students to walk their own path where curriculum is considered a journey to be discovered together not a standard that is written on the board to be achieved.

    Standard consensus necessitates that educators must be subject oriented; we need to be extremely knowledgeable in our chosen field of study. But is that enough? Do we also need to be good people? According to Henderson and Gornik, educators should indeed be concerned with and engaged in much more. "Educators should be encouraging their students to be both good and

---

49. Henderson and Gornik, *Transformative Curriculum Leadership.*

smart, and our reference for goodness are the democratic values of society. These values hold a society together and allow for the realization of the best in each person; therefore, these are the values that should be emphasized in education—particularly public education."[50] Curriculum wisdom focuses on cultivating values that endure the test of time. It requires the absolute commitment to asking the tough questions about content; such questions are deep with meaning about generosity, compassion, the good of all, who benefits, what does our community believe, will it last, does it make the world a better place. Moral wisdom does not come without complications; it is not a thing that you get. "It is not a thing, but a process; not singular, but plural; not static, but dynamic; not a technique, but an inquiring way of living."[51] To embark upon curriculum wisdom as an approach to curriculum development is to welcome transformative change.

There are several ways to interpret transformative change. Freire[52] refers to this transformative change as a type of praxis that was discussed in chapter 2 of this book. Dewey and Bentley's Theory of Inquiry[53] as interpreted by Ryan[54] requires that the habits of everyday teaching are disrupted by a problem, which promotes creating a hypothesis and seeking the tools and data required to go through transformative change; new habits are formed and a nonreflective state is sustained. Pinar refers to this personal change as *currere* defined as "complicated conversation with oneself (as a private intellectual), an ongoing project of self-understanding in which one becomes mobilized for engaged pedagogical action."[55] For our purposes and more specifically for teachers, *currere* offers the opportunity to embark upon a journey of change, for themselves and their colleagues with the possibility of changing society in the process. In order to undertake this intellectual leap,

50. Henderson and Gornik, *Transformative Curriculum Leadership*, 11.
51. Ibid., 12.
52. Freire, *Pedagogy of the Oppressed*.
53. Dewey and Bentley, *Knowing and the Known*.
54. Ryan, *Seeing Together*.
55. Pinar, *What is Curriculum Theory*, 37.

participants on this journey must question their place in the bigger picture. Finding this deep moral, ethical, and intellectual meaning is "fundamentally related to whether teachers are likely to find the considerable energy required to transform the status quo."[56] Teachers, who choose to be inspired leaders in their classrooms and in their buildings, choose then to guide others to find their path with a spirit of seeking wisdom, using the love of wisdom as a guide for "human freedom through expressions of reasonable, authentic self-direction."[57]

## 3S DESIGN

A component of curriculum wisdom is teaching with a 3S understanding, which can be used in the development of curriculum. Henderson and Gornik's definition of the 3S design is the "integration of subject matter understanding with democratic self and social understanding[58]" Teaching with the 3S design in mind encourages a quest for self-emancipation thus establishing a trust in sharing power relations with students as well. 3S empowers teachers through holistic understanding taking into account that students embark on their own individual journeys. This practice is a continually reflective study-based inquiry. Henderson and Gornik call this practice reflective inquiry, which requires asking questions while problem solving in curriculum development.

While I have studied this design for many years including in my doctoral research,[59] I struggle with the practical implementation of understanding subject matter with the *Common Core Standards* looming in our educational practices. How do teachers incorporate a 3S design that includes subject matter understanding with the present day standardized content? Do teachers really have any choice about curriculum which seems almost scripted in

---

56. Fullan, *New Meaning of Educational Change*, 39.
57. Henderson and Gornik, *Transformative Curriculum Leadership*, 21.
58. Ibid., 8.
59. Samford, "Exploring Sustained Change."

content and directed toward multiple examples of proper delivery? I remember when standards became state dictated several years back, and I recall thinking to myself that they can dictate the subject but we choose the delivery. Sadly, that is becoming less and less true as the how-to of teaching is slowly being federally removed. I struggle with incorporating the theoretical notion of deconstructing standards and the reality of mandated subject matter. Theory to practice elicits a present disparity that is heavy laden with the evils of our system today. On one hand, I want to encourage digging into standards with theory as a guide. Yet my practical experience rages at the audacity of what may be an unattainable goal, not to mention deviation from the standardized subject matter is directly linked to testing and ultimately, professional evaluation. So, the original question stands: How do we teach with a 3S design that includes subject matter integrated with democratic self and social understanding? One teacher that has used this approach to building curriculum stated her use of the 3S design this way:

> I received my "Teacher Leader" certification in the spring of 2012, with over a decade of teaching experience. I looked forward to being a lead learner and was determined to hit the ground running by totally overhauling my approach to lesson planning in the art room. I was particularly inspired by the concept of "wiggle room" from a book we had read called Motion Leadership. As an elementary art teacher, I felt little ability to effect measurable change in the building as a whole, let alone inspire a paradigm shift in curricular wisdom. Yet, Motion Leadership readings, and the inspiration of my program professors led me to invest in the concept of making little changes, things I could do, that might lead to later and bigger efforts.[60]

Donaldson refers to the term "wiggle room"[61] as the direction you can take when you step back, reflect, and rework an idea together to move forward in a constructive manner. Wiggle room

---

60. Lois Girbino, email message to author, January 25, 2015.
61. Donaldson, *How Leaders Learn*.

THE VASTNESS OF CURRICULUM DEVELOPMENT

is a place created through desire to find an alternative route for making progress in a position you deem worthwhile. Gleaning through the standards with a lens of self-discovery, what do we see? We see, inputting yourself into the subject relinquishes a variation of opinions thus deepening democratic meaning. We see individual understanding of divergence, disagreement, or even despair relinquishes feelings that provoke further investigation and questioning prior reasoning. We see a global social perspective opening opportunity for empathy of differing cultures. In summary, implementing a democratic self and social understanding of the 3S design into the teaching of subject matter allows opportunity for our standardized subject to bloom into a space for inquiry. Inquiry into democratic self and social understanding "paves the problem-solving path for us to be transformative teachers who treat their students as if they have minds of their own, encouraging them to use their mental capacities to build more sophisticated democratic understanding."[62] The idea of curriculum wisdom empowers teachers through inquiry and experience to re-imagining the self's journey and the journey of others.

## CONCLUSION

It is time to stand together; a time for taking on the problem of the standardized management paradigm while simultaneously focusing on a democratic form of curriculum development. We educators need to create a strong political opposition, standing together to fight the corruption of outside control over our schools. Whether through teacher unions or through a grass-roots effort encouraging parental participation, we are capable and responsible for eliciting the change needed to confront this problem.

In order for this vast change to take place in our school environment, we must build a Platform for Curriculum Development (PCD) to support a safe place for change to take place. This platform must be established in order for teachers to embark their

---

62. Henderson and Gornik, *Transformative Curriculum Leadership*, 53.

own *currere* and to support the change that needs to take place in our schools. Chapter 5 introduces this support system.

# 5

# A Platform for Curriculum Development

"Change will always fail until we find some way of developing infrastructure and processes that engage teachers in developing new knowledge, skills, and understandings."[1]

"Crucial is the recognition that conditions must be deliberately created to enable the mass of people to act on their power to choose."[2]

"If the stage is not set, people do not take the initiative to dialogue and silence is perpetuated. The leader, in this case the lead learner, cannot dictate theory but instead, grows with his or her colleagues. The lead learner sees this forging not in terms of explaining to, but rather dialoguing with the people."[3]

1. Fullan, *New Meaning of Educational Change,* 29.
2. Greene, *Dialectic of Freedom,* 88.
3. Freire, "Pedagogy of the Oppressed," 35.

Support for developing a curriculum wisdom paradigm does not currently exist in most public school settings. Many schools must rely on mandated content meetings to disseminate standardized expectations handed down from a state-level that is all too often tied to federal mandates. There is simply no time set aside to develop curriculum. I have spent many years applying theory and practice to come up with the necessary steps to support professional development or what I refer to for purposes of this chapter as a Platform for Curriculum Development (PCD). This chapter is a call for classroom teachers to push for a PCD and an expectation for teacher/administrators to accept the challenge of supporting that platform. In chapter 4 there was reference to brave teachers who close their doors and apply their best shot at teaching the *Common Core State Standards* creatively with added content of their own. We need to do more than to rely on some people to do the right thing, working around the fear of losing their livelihood. Even if these brave renegades succeed in "hit and miss" success, the tests still loom with a daunting force continuing to drive the content.

  Still fresh in my mind is a conversation that I had with my eleven-year-old stepson, leaving a recent weight of step-parent guilt. Evan asked to go to bed early because he wanted to make sure he had enough sleep, mind you this is a first at the Samford household. After feeling his forehead for a temperature, I asked him why he wanted to go to bed early. It was then, the night before testing, that he finally shared his feelings about the upcoming standardized tests. He shared that he was going to be tested every day for four days in a row; these were only four of eleven upcoming standardized tests expected of sixth graders in Ohio. After he said his prayers, he asked, "What will happen to me if I don't pass the test?" "Will you be mad at me?" I did my best to comfort him telling him that his dad and I care only about his effort not all about the results.

  I cannot help but wonder if his teachers, my prior colleagues, felt the same with their evaluations tied directly to his results. I can muster enough guilt to kill a lesser woman for not "opting" him and his sister out of the tests, but I know in my inner soul that opting out does not solve the bigger problem. My step-children would still be exposed daily to the mandated curriculum and excused only for the few hours that the testing takes place. Although the current parental movement to opt out of testing is making a worthwhile statement about over-reliance on testing, I think teachers have a different responsibility. As teachers, as wards of these children, we need to find the strength and fortitude to stop the invasion of our profession. I believe a PCD will support that momentum. "What we want is institutions that encourage the skill and the will to do the right thing."[4] Teachers need to band together to "change the law, not evade it"[5] for the betterment of all of our students.

## CREATING A PLATFORM

Creating a platform for change is very much like a making a garden. We work to clear the area of debris and move on to tilling the soil, laying the groundwork for growth. Seeds must then be planted and cared for regularly. However, there is no certainty that the seeds will grow and the garden will flourish. Many years back I planted seeds in an egg carton with my son in the late winter. We readied the garden in the early spring, working hard to create a lesson in science, fun memories, and, of course, a garden. As it turned out the lesson was, if you do not have a high enough fence deer will jump the fence and eat your garden. As every teacher knows, the biggest lessons are not always expected; the same is true with a platform. The result will not be exact because "knowledge is always becoming"[6] and the free will of a PCD eliciting personal and professional growth leaves a great deal of room for days when the deer will jump the fence. With change, it is imperative that there is a "valuing of creative tension associated with human interaction

---

4. Schwartz and Sharpe, *Practical Wisdom,* 234.
5. Ibid., 234.
6. Horton and Friere, *We Make the Road by Walking,* 101.

grounded in conflicting beliefs."[7] In other words, expect that you may need to replant your garden if it gets eaten on the first try.

It takes strong teachers willing to step up and combat the challenges to see this platform to fruition. Barth calls these teachers lead learners in the Foreword of Donaldson's book entitled, *How Leaders Learn*. According to Barth, lead learners can be described as such,

> "The world has begun to recognize that if schools are to significantly improve, it will be the resident practitioners who will improve them. And we have learned that most teachers and administrators have the capacity to develop and provide capable leadership to improve their schools—if the conditions are right. It remains for us to discover those conditions under which school practitioners become voracious, lifelong learners and accomplished leaders."[8]

Teachers who accept the challenge as a lead learners invoke the study of curriculum development[9] to not only become consumers of knowledge but also to become "active participants in conversations that they themselves will lead."[10] "The moral authority of the educational leader comes first and foremost from being a learner."[11] Engaging and inviting other "curriculum stakeholders to join in these studies as voluntary, collaborative partners"[12] is the goal and a continual challenge for lead learners. Lead learners are those who begin the challenge of accepting there is a problem that they refuse to perpetuate by habit and encouraging their colleagues to do the same. Lead learners are those pushing for an environment that supports a PCD to begin the discussions that need to take place. "Their growth—and that of their schools—comes from the creative tension between the ideal and the real, from the pebbles in

---

7. Henderson, "Curriculum Discourse," 207.
8. Donaldson, *How Leaders Learn*, ix.
9. Henderson, "Collegial Reflective Inquiry."
10. Pinar, *What is Curriculum Theory*, 33.
11. Barth, *How Leaders Learn*, x.
12. Henderson, "Teacher Leadership," 4.

their shoes that chafe when their own performance doesn't match what the school needs to grow."[13]

The drive for becoming a lead learner is an internal drive; teachers are intrinsically motivated. If focus for the inner drive of curriculum development rests on external motivations—positive or negative—it promotes a lack of interest when the goals are met; in other words, only the results become important. This is obvious with the recent, unsuccessful attempt at merit pay in education.[14] Intrinsic motivators work when the reward is the activity itself. Pink[15] suggests three elements to intrinsic motivation: 1) Autonomy—the desire to direct our own lives, 2) Mastery—the urge to make progress, get better and, 3) Purpose—the yearning to do something bigger than ourselves. Creating a PCD in today's public schools will require strong lead learners to step up and begin to take the journey for themselves, with their colleagues. Through engaging in research and by taking responsibility for professional growth, teachers can begin to seek their own democratic communities.[16] Leading for this type of growth requires the commitment of individuals that believe in the importance of social consciousness and are ready to participate in "critical reflective inquiry about problems and then commit to public actions that solve these problems."[17] It is time we take action for our own sake, for our students, and for our profession and its integrity.

## PLATFORM FOR CURRICULUM DEVELOPMENT

There are several purposes for building a Platform for Curriculum Development (PCD). Firstly, it has the potential to be a political catalyst to address how teachers regain control of subject matter and the evaluation of that subject matter. Secondly, it can be a safe

13. Donaldson, *How Leaders Learn*, 149.
14. Hargrove et al., "No Teachers Left Behind."
15. Pink, *Drive*.
16. Howard and Parker, "Resisting Silence."
17. Hackney and Henderson, "Develop the Instructional Leadership," 107.

environment to begin to discuss what curriculum means to us as individuals, as schools, as communities, and as a society. Thirdly, it encourages and supports our *currere* and that of our colleagues and serves as an example of a platform for our classroom to support the 3S journey of our students. There are many examples of ideas on how to set up professional development,[18] learning communities,[19] staff development,[20] but what ever language is used, researching these theories for professional development can be daunting. It took me seven years of researching theories and conducting professional development to define a PCD, and how I understand it continues to be developed today. Presently, a PCD elicits administrative support to make time to develop trust thus promoting collegiality that expects sustained change grounded in democratic values to support curriculum development. Each of these topics: administrative support, time, trust, collegiality, change, democratic values and curriculum development has been thoroughly researched to be an integral and necessary ingredient in the development of a successful PCD.

*Administrative support.* Administrative support is unequivocally necessary for the success of sustaining change in the school setting.[21] Whether we are credentialed teachers or later, credentialed administrators, every administrative certificate suggests having three years of successful teaching experience. In this section, I call upon administrative support to make time for a PCD and further clarify that we are all teachers first and foremost. Lead learners also play a role in the development of this platform to support administrators and colleagues in initiating an environment conducive to the success of this platform. "Leadership not only matters, it is second only to teaching among school related factors in its

18. Guskey, "What Makes Professional Development."
19. Lovett and Gilmore, "Teachers' Learning Journeys."
20. Filho, "Teaching Sustainable Development."
21. Samford, Caster, Gornik, and Henderson, "Teachers and Administrators."

impact."[22] In their executive summary, Leithwood, Seashore, Anderson, and Wahlstrom explore the influence of leadership concluding that school reform is not possible without high-quality leaders thus "providing teachers and others in the system with the necessary support and training to succeed."[23] Aligning with such an idea, DuFour acknowledges as an administrator he has "come to understand that the most significant contribution a principal can make to developing others is creating an appropriate context for adult learning."[24]

One resounding result of my doctoral studies and research was administrators can make or break an initiative in a building.[25] Repeatedly, participants in my study reported that if they had the support of their administrator, they saw success in their initiatives, and participants immediately saw the opposite result if that support was non-existent or removed. In order for the initiative to be developed, administrators elicited the support of teachers in that change. The best leaders know that you must involve all participants in a given context in order to initiate change; we go further and achieve more when working together.[26] Put another way, new practice "emerges from the interactions among people and their situation, rather than as a function of the actions of any one individual leader."[27] Although the administrator is a necessary ingredient in setting up the PCD, they then become one of the lead learners.

Administrators and lead learners together support the creation of the environment in the school building to make the initiative possible. Setting the tone for deep cultures that work on "purposeful, continuous learning"[28] establishes "legacy

22. Perrone, "Reflections on Teaching," 637.
23. Leithwood et al., "How Leadership Influences," 3.
24. DuFour, "In the Right Context," 14.
25. Samford, "Exploring Sustained Change."
26. Spillane, "Engaging Practice," 201–219.
27. Ibid., 209.
28. Fullan, *What's Worth Fighting for*, 19.

conditions" that insure "continuity of good direction."[29] Leaders can make a profound difference in the performance of their organizations when they ask, "What is the moral imperative?"[30] The PCD that our teacher/administrators need to build are "boundary-defying entities that are unthreatened and uncontrolled by bureaucracies."[31] Leaders who strive to build a PCD in their buildings know that "the best of leaders when the job is done, when the task is accomplished, the people will all say we have done it ourselves."[32] That is leadership.

*Time.* One of the difficulties that might occur in moving to this type of platform in schools is time management. Immediate problems are inevitable in the school setting so we spend time brainstorming "practical solutions to resolve immediate problems."[33] Anyone working in the field of education knows that things move at the speed of light. When I initially transferred to the middle school setting as a building administrator, I remember laughing, a lot. I do not mean in a quiet type of demeanor but the kind where the laugh bellows out at a time that is possibly inappropriate and definitely not controlled. I kept asking the administrative assistants, "Is it always like this?" to which they would say simultaneously, "Yes!" Surviving while thriving in the education of pre-pubescent students leaves little time for initiatives, of this I am aware. However, time is something that is in our control and must be stolen from any available corner for trust to be developed. Making deep change such as developing new teaching skills, approaches, conceptions to the very nature of educational philosophy will take longer to achieve than that of federally mandated change. Of course, if you support the time for this holistic change, it "will have a greater impact once accomplished."[34] Not to mention allowing

---

29. Ibid., 19.
30. Reeves, "Level-Five Networks," 249.
31. Ibid., 249.
32. Horton and Freire, *We Make the Road by Walking*, 248.
33. Slattery, *Curriculum Development*, 237.
34. Fullan, *New Meaning of Educational Change*, 36.

time to keep up with one's field avoids "intellectual deskilling" and over-reliance on processes provided by "experts."[35]

Schwartz and Sharpe[36] condense a study conducted at a seminary by J. M. Darley and C. D. Batson[37] in which theological students were told they had to give a lecture on the parable of the Good Samaritan[38] The students were told they were already late and were required to leave the classroom immediately to attend a seminar in the next building. As they rushed off, a man was slumped in an ally with his head down, obviously in need of assistance. Only 10 percent of the seminary students stopped to help. In a different study, the seminarians were told they had time before the lecture but they had to go to the next building. As they passed the man in the alley, 63 percent of the seminary students stopped to help. The point is, if we have time, we feel empathy and trust our intuition. Any program or in our case educational institutions "can fail to provide the necessary evolutionary support by neglecting to build a bridge out of and beyond the old world, it can also fail by expecting its charges to take up immediate residence in the new world."[39] When building an environment for a PCD, people need time to feel comfortable working together.

Walker[40] studied the way people work in groups, what they discuss, how they share their point of view or their thoughts on a subject, and how they move forward on topics. People spend time talking about their beliefs, laying the groundwork for their curricular views. It is only through the venue of time that trust is developed. Through discussion, persuasion, problem solving, and weighing all information presented, people deliberate to reach the best course of action, and thus altering their original curricular platform. Maslow[41] contended that only breathing, food, water,

35. Apple, *Ideology and Curriculum,* 189.
36. Schwartz and Sharpe, *Practical Wisdom.*
37. Darley and Batson, "From Jerusalem to Jericho," 100–108.
38. Luke, *Bible,* 10:25–37.
39. Kegan, *In Over Our Heads,* 46.
40. Walker, "Process of Curriculum Development."
41. Maslow, "Theory of Human Motivation."

sleep, and excretion come before physical and emotional safety as a need. We have to trust that we will not be harmed in order to move to higher level thinking.

    Years ago, I initiated a program of co-teaching in our district. Principals, prospective general education co-teachers, prospective intervention specialists, and I visited several schools to see what various districts had in place. We took the time that was needed to visit area schools and always set aside time for lunch and time to debrief, brainstorming our thoughts on a plan for our individual buildings. I had not counted on the animosity that was to follow. One teacher had commented several times throughout the trips that the initiative would never work in that particular building. The same teacher made a comment about special education teachers not having "real authority" in the classroom. Later, one intervention specialist from that building whispered to me, "I love the idea of co-teaching, but you will have a hard time getting past her." Although we took the time to develop the co-teaching initiative, time alone is not enough. An atmosphere of trust must exist for people to publicly disclose their private thoughts.

*Trust.* Fullan[42] supported two conditions that are a necessity for success in professional development. The first ingredient is structural, taking the time to meet and to communicate. The second need is social, a culture that must exist in trust and respect. There is a great deal of research on the importance of social culture, but Lumpe[43] in particular supports research-based professional development encouraging time and trust to engage in meaningful collaboration. Burbank and Kauchak also felt people need time to develop trust for meaningful dialogue and reflective inquiry; "collaboration requires trust and sharing."[44]

    In a heartwarming dialogue from a group of teacher leaders, trust was described as a "give and take."[45] Susan School—one of

    42. Fullan, *What's Worth Fighting for.*
    43. Lumpe, "Research Based Professional Development."
    44. Burbank and Kauchak, "Alternative Model," 512.
    45. Griest et al., "Lead Learning Stories," 161.

the teacher leaders—went on to elaborate on this idea by stating "trust isn't a free gift; it's earned. It's something that you have to establish within a relationship. Relationship and trust, I think, go together."[46] Konni Stagliano, another teacher leader, echoed the connection between trust and relationships and went on to share her feeling of trust with an administrator she works beside in her building.

> I felt her trust, which might not be the case for all teachers. I know I'm given trust from her; I feel I can do more in my classroom and I won't be criticized for it because of trust. I can take the trust I have received and put it into my classroom and allow my students to feel that trust from me. I think trust needs to be extended from colleague to colleague as well. If they don't feel you're honest and trustworthy, then why are they going to believe in you or share with you or learn with you?[47]

Time to develop trust elicits empathy for each other; it opens our minds and our hearts to the possibility of new beginnings. With trust, we also open ourselves to the possibility of constructive criticism; empathy invites differing opinions with the trust that the critique is not for harm but for the betterment of all.

I have a vivid memory of walking down the hall and seeing a student slumped over sitting outside of a closed door. As was my common practice, I sat on the floor next to the student and asked her what was wrong. Through tears, the student shared that she had spent a good part of the night with her mom and siblings visiting her brother in jail. Needless to say, she did not do her homework packet. I knocked on the door and shared the information with the teacher—who was exemplary in her teaching, in her attitude, and in her respect toward her colleagues and her students. When I shared with her the plight of her student, she almost ran to the hall and hugged the student. She immediately apologized to her student for being short tempered and explained that she had a bad morning. The demeanor of this student immediately changed.

46. Ibid., 161.
47. Ibid., 161.

## Out of the Dark

Tears turned to an aura of joy, and the student promised to have the packet the following day. I do not know if that student did the homework the next day or not, but I do know that the trust that the teacher had with me and the empathy she had for her student, immediately changed that situation. There was no mistrust on the part of the teacher, she knew was not being judged. We simply took time to listen to a student, and because I had already developed trust with the teacher, there was no animosity.

In the prior example of the teacher that was making derogatory comments about the co-teaching initiative coming to her building, I spent a great deal of time that year working with the teacher to develop trust for the co-teaching initiative and trust in me as a colleague. That teacher was well read, highly intelligent, and passionate about teaching. I offered her unlimited material on co-teaching, had many high-level conversations, and eventually she helped plan and implement the co-teaching program in her building. As a result of taking time to build this trust, this general education co-teacher became a positive proponent of co-teaching in our district until her retirement.

*Colleagiality.* The Merriam Webster Dictionary defines collegiality as "the cooperative relationship of colleagues," interestingly, the same source defines cooperative as "two or more people or groups working together to do something" and relationship as "the way in which two or more people, groups, countries, etc., talk to, behave toward, and deal with each other."[48] These definitions have no correlation to a friendly "Hello" in the hallway, a brief talk about course content, or a quick check of where a fellow content teacher is in the curriculum map. Collegiality speaks of people working together in a certain manner to accomplish a goal. Although the talk of curriculum mapping, policy mandates, or standardized test data is very much a part of teachers lives, developing collegiality for a 3S design "is more inquiry, a fundamental generating of points of entry, and practical and collective transactions to prompt

---

48. Merriam Webster Dictionary, "collegiality" and "cooperative."

further development of holistic understanding."[49] As one teacher explained, "the substance of 3S collegial study stands in stark contrast toward much of the professional training that takes place today."[50] Rich collaboration that leads to collegiality is a necessary ingredient for PCD.

The term coined "professional learning communities" came on the scene in the 1980's with the main component being implementing collaboration in the school setting.[51] In countless studies, collaboration and collegiality continuously top the checklist for creating an atmosphere for learning in the teaching profession.[52] Phrases supporting collegiality among staff members at the building level were cited as "a major support mechanism for the continued learning by teachers interviewed."[53] In another study engaging in professional discourse with like-minded colleagues deepened knowledge of subject matter while prompting collegiality.[54] The research supporting collegiality in a school environment is undeniable.

The opposite is true if collegiality is not developed.[55] If teachers do not have the opportunity to reflect on practice with others, any inadequacies in that practice are overlooked, buried. When the necessity for collegial conversation is overlooked, constructive criticism is absent. People must be able to trust in a collegial atmosphere that they can critique the work of others and expose their own errors to secure the growth of their colleagues. Collegiality can only exist with the common knowledge that "public disclosure of private errors will not lead to their suffering negative consequences."[56] Only then can an open dialogue develop. Coop-

49. Fishman, "Sowing Holistic Understanding," 78.

50. Ibid., 78.

51. DuFour, "What is a Professional Learning Community."

52. Smith and Gillespie, "Research on Professional Development." King and Newman, "Building School Capacity."

53. Engstrom and Danielson, "Teachers' Perceptions," 172.

54. Feiman-Nemser, "From Preparation to Practice."

55. Brookfield, *Becoming a Critically Reflective Teacher*.

56. Ibid., 250.

erating with other teachers to re-think curriculum development necessitates all contributors to offer completely candid opinions. When this occurs, so does empowerment; people are able to speak and act according to their true beliefs. One powerful ingredient for change in schools is collaborative inquiry as "deep and productive professional learning is critical to educational change."[57] With a platform for the growth of collegiality in place, teachers have time to act mindfully rather than react out of old habit. This proactive agenda quickly becomes a strong agent for change.

*Change.* Using a transactional approach to developing curriculum theory accepts, and expects variations, no one truth. Transaction challenges a one answer, linear, scientific approach to thinking about problems and situations.[58] Dewey's and Bentley's work in, *Knowing and the Known* describes transaction as "a collection of useful yet fallible human practices open to ongoing modification."[59] Visualize all participants contributing with small pieces of a truth, on-going and never settling on one overall truth, rather consistently re-creating bits of truth for that moment in time. Accepting this philosophical theory of combining ideas is about creating a pathway to mutual acceptance until another change becomes necessary. Fully accepting a problem as "solved" is not a goal. Ultimately, change is the only constant.

Teachers are experts at incremental changes that occur in the classroom on a daily basis. When teachers have a platform for discussing, aligning, and developing curriculum needs, there is a deep awareness of the issue at hand and new ideas for renewal are possible. In other words, a PCD provides the safety net to allow educators to change, create temporary resolutions as they are sure to develop in the classroom, and then discuss those changes with their colleagues. This can be liberating as teachers no longer would be forced to absorb a pre-existing reality but would have the authority to shape curriculum. This would position teachers as

57. Earl, "Accountability as a Collective Professional Responsibility," 103.
58. Ryan, *Seeing Together.*
59. Ibid., 39.

being "in control of our issues rather than having our issues be in control of us."[60]

Fifteen years ago I had the opportunity to move from a classroom to a central office position. This is quite a drastic learning curve and my superintendent was kind and met with me often as I struggled to make major decisions for the district. Weighing all options for students and teachers while applying the legal and financial restraints was stifling my decision-making process. Then, one fine day my superintendent looked up from his desk and simply said to me, "Wendy, it is easier to beg forgiveness than ask permission." This small statement was enough to let me know I had permission to make my own decisions and forgiveness when I would inevitably make mistakes. I was instantly empowered to handle changes as they occurred in a timely manner. Because he supported me, I went on to motivate my colleagues, working together to make many influential changes in our district. "How to activate individual and peer motivation on a large scale is the holy grail of change,"[61] and I believe this motivation is internal, innate in lead learners but the missing ingredient for change is a platform to support it. Can we learn to embrace growth, expect change, and demand a venue that is grounded in democratic values?

*Democratic Values:* Grounding a PCD in democratic values sounds like a lofty goal. It requires that we think of our colleagues, fellow teachers, as equal contributors to the issue at hand. It requires that we are not formulating our opinion, busily thinking about our contribution but, instead, valuing the opinion of our colleagues to see their possible influence on our own ideas. "To resist immediate desires in favor of those that possess long-term benefits"[62] for the good of all requires the ability to self-regulate. Self-regulation sometimes means waiting to form our own opinion as well as waiting for others to form theirs; put another way, it means valuing

---

60. Kegan, *In Over Our Heads,* 133.
61. Fullan, *Leading Educational Change,* xii.
62. DeSteno, *Truth About Trust,* 25.

both opinions as equally important in the democratic process for the good of all.

One of my favorite research studies was done at Stanford Universities Bing Nursery School in 1960; it was called simply "The Marshmallow Test."[63] Grossly simplifying, preschool children in this study had a choice, they could have one marshmallow immediately or, if they waited, they could have two. The researchers then followed the lives of these students. The more seconds the student waited before eating the marshmallow in preschool, "the higher their SAT scores and the better their related social and cognitive functioning in adolescence."[64] By the time the participants reached their late-20s and early-30s, those that waited for two marshmallows had a lower body mass index, better sense of self-efficacy, and coped better with stress. This study supports the value in waiting, the self-control of not reacting immediately. It supports the long-term benefits to valuing our ability to delay gratification in order to reach higher goals. This is important because it is imperative that we allow the wait time necessary for our thoughts and the thoughts of our colleagues to grow, trusting that something better will come by valuing this democratic process.

Gail Saunders-Smith[65] was invited to come to our district as part of a professional development initiative to support guided reading. It was a tedious in-service to set up as she rotated through four different elementary buildings twice, and all teachers had to be pulled from the classroom by grade level to witness a guided reading circle. The logistics involved setting the teachers schedules and securing substitute teachers to rotate to different classes as grade level teachers attended the in-service—not to mention grouping kids by similar reading levels and pulling them from class. Doing all of this was no easy task. During the demonstrations, I distinctly remember Dr. Saunders-Smith asking a question about the definition of a vocabulary word to one first grade boy. He moved nervously in his seat, sat on his hands, looked at the

---

63. Mischel, *The Marshmallow Test*.
64. Ibid., 5.
65. Saunders-Smith, *Ultimate Guided Reading*.

## A Platform for Curriculum Development

page, and started rocking. Yet, she waited. The other children just sat there looking at their books; there was complete silence. The teachers in the room grew uncomfortable, but still, the wait time continued. She worded the question a different way attempting to scaffold the young student to the answer. Still there was no answer.

My administrative brain was on fire. "What is she doing? Why is she waiting so long? Why would she not ask another student to help this poor boy? It took me forever to set this up and she is wasting time. Plus, we have another rotation of teachers coming. We will not get to the end of this reading passage." After a horribly long wait, the boy shot out a definition that was beyond any expectation. Everyone in the room broke out in spontaneous clapping, relief that the tension stopped, but more importantly that he shared such a high-level answer with his fellow classmates. He needed time. Because Dr. Saunders-Smith valued his opinion so highly and, after all, it was his turn, that little reading group got so much more than if he had been passed over. I have never forgotten that lesson. This example illustrates the importance of valuing the voices and opinions of everyone as "all have value incommensurably, absolutely, and infinitely."[66]

Maybe this seems idealistic, grounding our platform in democracy, but it must begin with the absolute value of individuals contributing to the overall cause. Democracy means "neither death or life has any value in and of itself, but that value comes from shared existence."[67] The belief must be in the power of people coming together to take responsibility individually and together for the process of the platform. Maxine Greene states her hope of "freedom in dialogue with others for the sake of personal fulfillment and the emergence of a democracy dedicated to life and decency,"[68] and this sounds almost out of reach. Our present day focus seems to be on the over importance of individualism, the belief in our own power. The strength of the United States of America comes from individuals joining forces, accepting, recog-

---

66. Nancy, *Truth of Democracy,* 24.
67. Ibid., 31.
68. Greene, *Dialectic of Freedom,* xii.

nizing, and valuing differences. When teachers join together "reinforcing each other's differences"[69] it stimulates creativity and we gain strength. This experience in acceptance initiates innovation. Teachers do their ultimate best in this time of standardization to provide a classroom atmosphere that supports all students' ideas, valuing all opinions. Why would we, as teachers, not expect this atmosphere for ourselves? Is curriculum development a topic that is worth fighting for?

*Curriculum Development:* A PCD necessitates creating the environment to support the important initiative of developing curriculum. I call your attention back to the opening quote from chapter 4:

> What do schools teach, what should they teach, and who should decide? Is the primary aim of education to instill basic skills or foster critical thinking? Should education aim to mold future citizens, transmit national values, engender personal development or inspire academic achievement? Must education have an aim? And what beliefs, values or attitudes are learned from the way classrooms are? That is, what lessons are taught but not planned, acquired but taken for granted?[70]

There are many more questions asked than answers given in developing curriculum. Think about your own classroom; how many of these questions do you ask and address daily, monthly, and annually? *Common Core State Standards* aside, teachers have the ability to direct self and social understanding thus affecting the democratic the growth of their students. The 3S design for curriculum development[71] challenges educators to transition and embrace curriculum wisdom while utilizing problem solving techniques. This design challenges lead learners to embrace wisdom for problem solving and reflective inquiry. And I feel so many teachers are ready and hungry for this challenge.

69. Ibid., 52.
70. Flinders and Thornton, *Curriculum Studies Reader*, xi.
71. Henderson and Gornik, *Transformative Curriculum Leadership*.

## A Platform for Curriculum Development

It seems as though educators have lost the power to develop local curriculum. Control over subject matter seems no longer under local influence and slowly it follows that we may be losing the ability to teach the subject matter in a manner we feel is best for students. As discussed in chapter 4, consistency over subject matter can be useful. Consistent subject matter is an outline of what we, the professional experts in our field, feel is important for our students to know about the subjects taught. Teaching subject matter consistently is not the enemy; forcibly dictated, specifically stated "how" to teach and what results are acceptable to be regurgitated on multiple standardized tests is very much the enemy. Imagine the worthwhile endeavor of developing our own curriculum that advances a problem-solving approach that integrates subject understandings that are integrated with democratic self and social understandings. It is time to take back responsibility for our professional right to be the authority in our own field of education. What does this specifically look like? How do we begin?

## CONCLUSION

This chapter illustrated the importance of developing lead learners, the shared importance of creating an environment to support change, and defined a PCD that elicits administrative support to make time to develop trust thus promoting collegiality that expects sustained change grounded in democratic values to support curriculum development. Although the PCD definition was well researched, theory is only half of the battle in education; we must also apply that theory to practice lest it remain untested.

In the next chapter, schools that have taken on the challenge of change in their buildings and work toward creating their own rendition of educational renewal are explored. Theirs is a hermeneutic compilation of creative curriculum design while embracing a collegial, empowering environment. Examples of schools that incorporate theory into practice completely encapsulating the meaning of democracy into their campuses are highlighted in chapter 6. These are schools that are taking on the challenge of educational renewal in the present-day standardized management paradigm. One idea is not valued over the next; they are simply and democratically seeking to discover the best educational philosophy available for their students in their local communities.

# 6

# Renewal

"Spiritual, affective, and intellectual connections in the lives of educators working together to understand and improve their practice."[1]

"If we want change, we'll have to put up with the non-conformity and some messiness . We'll have to allow those most involved (teachers, administrators, parents) to exercise greater on-site power to put their collective wisdom into practice."[2]

Embracing renewal, working together to connect our lives to the lives of those we influence, is not about a short-term fix. Renewal is not about fixing at all, but nurturing change in the structure of education. And I hope to see and be a part of it in my lifetime. The first two chapters of this book focused on how we arrived in this standardized management paradigm and what keeps us engrained in this unsolicited invasion of the control over

---

1. Sirotnik, "Making Sense of Educational Renewal," 607–608.
2. Meier, *Power of Their Ideas,* 104.

curriculum in our local schools. The three chapters that followed illustrated the theories behind curriculum development, sustaining change, and a platform to support that change. This chapter will look at the application of theories and how schools are accepting the challenge of experimenting with curriculum development through a democratic process in their own journeys of understanding.

When thinking of renewal and cultivating democratic ways of being in our schools, I am reminded of a student I had during my first year of teaching. Although he carried a low "F" for the semester, I know he was listening because when I called upon him he always had an insightful answer. His sense of humor was far beyond his years, and over time, I surmised he was highly intelligent. There had to be more to this young man than the grades were showing so I recruited him to be part of the "technology team," which was responsible for transporting equipment to different teachers in the building. My thought was to trust him in hopes he would develop confidence and trust in me that would transfer over to his learning, eventually enabling him find some success in the classroom. Unfortunately, the last time I saw him, his hands were being held behind his back as he was being escorted from the building. I never saw him again as shortly thereafter I left that district to accept an administrative position. I cannot help but feel I failed that young man. How could I have reached out in a different way? How could our school have dug deeper to uncover his emotional intelligence[3] in areas not apparent in classroom material? Sixteen years later, I still think about that young man.

A career as an educator is not for the faint of heart. Teachers know that the true differences they make in the lives of their students are not quantifiable. Sirotnik describes a call for teaching as such:

> If you have a high tolerance for ambiguity and like to mess around with too many variables (and interactions) to measure (or measure well), with interventions or "treatments" that are usually ill defined and often hopelessly

---

3. Goleman, *Emotional Intelligence*.

confounded with others, with social/political/economic/ organizational contexts that are always colliding and changing, with ideological wars around what ought to be the very purposes and functions of the enterprise you think you are studying, and with pages and pages of text that represent what you see, what people write, and what people say in these settings that are engaged in long-term processes of renewal and change well then, have I got a career for you![4]

There are many schools that are trying new and exciting ideas to support curriculum development in a variety of ways with one commonality, devotion to and embodiment of democratic ideals. This chapter highlights a few of those schools in order to prompt discussion in building platforms with the intent to ignite a spark for exodus from controlled, mandated curriculum. As discussions promote change in education, let us open our minds to some big ideas that may initiate interest for change in our own buildings and thus in the lives of our students. The philosophies presented here for beginning conversations in curriculum development include: democratic principles as a focus for professional development, the power of choice, theme schools, and a kinder, more nurturing approach to education.

## EMBRACING DEMOCRATIC PROFESSIONAL DEVELOPMENT

In order to support the necessary growth mindset for teachers to embrace curriculum development, a Platform for Curriculum Development (PCD) must be developed. Years ago, as a beginning building administrator, I wanted to initiate a platform for conducting professional development in my new building. For years my building administrator had one meeting a month for special education teachers to schedule IEP parent meetings. Although this regimented meeting was necessary for scheduling IEP dates, as special education numbers grew it became apparent that we

4. Sirotnik, "Making Sense of Educational Renewal," 610.

needed to implement a Response to Intervention (RtI) program in our building. After many discussions with my colleagues over the next year, we gained approval to create forms to be used as referrals in our building. Created with the building principal, guidance counselors, teachers, and myself these forms were then shared in a small group format with all the teachers. Discussions over the purpose of RtI, the direction of intervention, and the frustration of increased numbers of our special education population were several topics on the agenda. Over the following year, the monthly RtI meetings were added to the building agenda. The meetings were attended regularly by the assistant principal, school psychologist, speech therapist, guidance counselors, and all special education teachers. Later in the year, one teacher representative from the referring team was asked to attend and speak on behalf of the child being discussed for RtI. The agenda was informal and relied on qualitative information gathered on each student. Specific notes obtained on each child were distributed prior to the meeting to allow information to be assimilated well in advance so each attendee arrived well informed. The forum was an open, democratic process developed over time with dialogue of honest opinions. Trust was a key ingredient of the forum; they knew their opinions were confidential and their words were valued. We did not always agree but we always moved forward for what we believed to be the best outcome for the children. Through reflective inquiry and problem solving, we cultivated ways to make this platform productive.

 Deborah Meier knows the importance of creating this platform and created several schools dedicated to empowering teachers and students that encapsulated the very sense of democracy. The superintendent in East Harlem's District 4 invited Meier to open a small elementary school in the wing of P.S. 171 so in 1974, she began a small pilot public school in East Harlem aimed at creating "an intense adult community of learners that will entice kids to want to belong too."[5] School District 4 served "one of the city's poorest communities" and "was educationally on the bottom, with

---

 5. Meier, *In Schools We Trust*, 30.

test scores that placed it last out of thirty-two city districts."[6] Her focus was to organize this school around collective decision making among teachers; each teacher was held responsible for his or her own work as well as the work of their colleagues. This common community of individuals came together with a deeper sense of creating a school tied into a restoration of democratic public life. Democratic "changes are required in schooling both in curriculum and pedagogy, what and how—above all in the relationships of learners to teachers, teachers to families, and teachers to each other."[7] One of the key places we learn the art of democracy, that is living together as citizens, in schools. When children are in the company of adults that they trust and see a democratic approach to learning, they are inclined to trust that democracy is possible and realize their voices are important. All people should have a voice "not only in their own work, but in the work of others as well."[8]

Creating a democratic environment takes time because teachers have to develop trust in each other. Meier knew that if teachers were being asked to take on the vast responsibility of thinking like an administrator, i.e., being responsible for their work and the work of others, they needed time to do so. The extra work involved in "intimately being a part of and responsible for the conduct of the whole school, from designing curriculum to evaluating colleagues"[9] requires accountability and accountability requires time. When time is taken to develop this environment, one byproduct is trust. Building trust allows people to count on each other for improvement always "keeping in mind the interests of the whole school—including what's happening to the kids across the hall."[10] When this atmosphere was developed, their school began to grow together. Casual comments of what one person was learning from another began to flow. This "work in prog-

---

6. Meier, *Power of Their Ideas*, 19.
7. Meier, *In Schools We Trust*, 19.
8. Meier, *Power of Their Ideas*, 22.
9. Meier, *In Schools We Trust*, 32–33.
10. Ibid., 61.

ress" defends the time it takes to create a democratic platform for curriculum development; after all, "what is at stake is defending how important it is to take one's ideas seriously enough to insist that they be heard."[11]

Over the years, Meier's school has multiplied into four schools in Harlem in the same district, and these schools are successful and are used as a positive example of restructuring public schools.[12] Keeping the focus on creating environments where kids and adults can "experience the power of their ideas" requires teachers to talk about the purpose of schooling.[13] They are developing curriculum that asks the tough "why" questions. This means teachers agree to accept "the responsibility for the shared future of the next generation."[14] In accepting this responsibility, the test scores in these four schools have risen, but more importantly, each school offers curriculum that is "full of powerful ideas and experiences aimed at inspiring its students with the desire to know more, a curriculum that sustains students' natural drive to make sense of the world and trust in their capacity to have an impact upon it."[15] A few of the lessons learned from this experience were: 1) an administrator is a necessary ingredient in the success of the building; 2) conflict is to be expected and it needs to be faced head on; 3) no one perfectly crafted solution to curriculum exists and; 4) schools must be built on respect and democracy and these take time and patience to build trust.

It is unfortunate we have not taken the information we have learned from this successful endeavor to creatively develop more schools based on the premise of democracy. When I contacted Deborah Meier, she mentioned the following statement and from her insights; it seems like we, as educational stakeholders, have some work to do.

11. Ibid., 75.
12. Fliegel and MacGuire, *Miracle in East Harlem*.
13. Meier, *Power of Their Ideas*, 4.
14. Ibid., 4.
15. Ibid., 16.

> We learn from the company we keep. In fact, it's the primary way all animals learn. So it behooves us to ask what it is that children between ages 4–18 see of the adult world—how they think it works. They spend a lot of time in a world in which teachers and other school staff interact. What they too often discover is that being an adult allows one to be disrespectful of those lower in status, to be fearful of those higher in the status, and gives them very little picture of what goes on when teachers gather together without their bosses. They become aware that teachers are not making the decisions that count, and that's "just the way it is." In short, they are not keeping company with adults who are attractive for their smarts, their creativity, their power, their collegiality, or their courage—all of which are hall marks of a democratic citizenship as well as just plain adultness of the kind the young might yearn to become.[16]

Our students are not only learning from the subjects that we teach, they are learning how to be productive adults in a democratic society. Are we, as teachers, a good example of a strong participant in a democratic society? Should we choose to set a different example?

## THE POWER OF CHOICE

Choice theory presumes that all behavior is always an attempt to satisfy at least one of five basic needs: 1) stay alive, 2) belonging, 3) power, 4) freedom, and 5) fun. In applying choice theory to education, "a good school could be defined as a place where almost all students believe that if they do some work, they will be able to satisfy their needs enough so that it makes sense to keep working."[17] The motivating drive for this force is internal as we would always be trying to satisfy one of these needs. Thus, learning is thought to be internally motivated not externally caused. Think about students today. Do they have any power over their learning, daily choice connected to their interests? According to

16. Deborah Meier, email message to author, April 7, 2015.
17. Glasser, *Choice Theory*, 16.

William Glasser, "the more students can fulfill their needs in your academic classes, the more they will apply themselves to what is to be learned."[18] And the opposite of this is if their needs are not met, they will become frustrated and gain attention in other ways. The teacher utilizing the choice approach to learning would be more of a facilitator, a coach where "all players experience not only power but also a strong sense of belonging."[19] Teachers are thus coaching this team effort, it is "their responsibility to restructure their teaching so that it is more satisfying"[20] for them and their students. This theory requires teaching to look like a learning-team model rather than a traditional model. The more teachers act "as facilitators, resource people, and coaches, the more they will find that the students in learning teams take much more responsibility now for their own education."[21] Power in such an approach is shared rather than reserved for and controlled by a very small group of individuals.

Alfred Adler—a physician and psychotherapist—studied children's behavior and spent a lifetime looking at the socialization of children and how to support their development. Like John Dewey in one sense, Adler "saw education as a direct function of a child's socialization and expression of democratic living. Adler wanted school to be a livable environment for children."[22] In promoting positive behavior in the school environment, Adler believed a healthy relationship with the child must first be established. His theory promotes truly understanding and investigating a child's life, interpreting the child's innate goals, and constructively designing those goals to support the development of a fully conceptualized human being.[23] When combining Adler's theory of

18. Ibid., 33.
19. Ibid., 75.
20. Ibid., 89.
21. Ibid., 90.
22. Dwornik, "A comparison of Educational Theory," 55.
23. Gamble and Watkins, "Combining the Child."

supporting goals with Glasser's choice theory, "a highly effective, comprehensive"[24] approach to education can be established.

Alfred Adler Elementary School in St. Petersburg, Florida was established on the basis of children setting goals and adults guiding their paths. All teachers use the book "Maintaining Sanity in the Classroom: Classroom Management Techniques"[25] as a resource for implementing the theory and the methods of Alfred Adler. Rather than obedience, cooperation and contribution are valued above all. Goals are established that "foster scholarly attainment, creativity, respectful and fulfilling social relationships, joy in learning and the development of caring citizens."[26] All decisions are based on choices. Traditional standards or punishment to control is not accepted with the belief that creativity is stifled if a child is afraid. At this school social interest and a feeling of belonging in society stimulates students to contribute to the welfare of everyone, increasing their own abilities while simultaneously contributing to those of the group.

Greg and Lori DeCosmo created this school eight years ago with Adler's philosophy central to the curriculum and basic philosophy of the school. This K-5 building believes there are two behaviors, useful and useless. Useful behavior is "cooperative action for the common good"[27] The opposite is true for useless behavior, it moves a person "toward promoting the self" not with the common good. In a phone conversation with me, Greg DeCosmo referred to an example of "freedom choices."[28] Children in Alfred Adler Elementary School understand they have freedom to make choices, and the adults that they are surrounded by at the school listen to, take seriously, and respect the choices children make.

For example, there are two bathroom passes, one male and one female in each classroom. Pass time is not limited but used

24. Ibid., 156.
25. Dreikurs et al., *Maintaining Sanity in the Classroom*.
26. Ibid., vii.
27. Ibid., 14.
28. Greg DeCosmo (entrepreneur) in discussion with the author, April 7, 2015.

with respect for the group as a whole. If, for instance, someone takes the pass and talks extensively at the drinking fountain and by the time they return their friend is in dire need of the restroom, that student negatively affected another person in the group. This action may prompt a classroom meeting to discuss in a democratic format, what the action of that student caused.

The school is set up in a cooperative structure where the teacher and the students manage the classroom. Together they strive for complete social equity based on a democratic classroom where "consideration for the other's rights and interests while standing up for one's own rights."[29] The goal is an established environment of mutual respect. Every student is recognized as contributing to the bigger picture unless the rights of others are being forfeited. Greg DeCosmo shared, "If Johnny wants to sing and dance during reading, they have to leave the classroom. They always want to come back because that is where their friends are and they want to be social and belong."[30] The teacher in a democratic classroom has the right and responsibility to give directions; put another way, a teacher assists each child in increasing their ability to take part in a group setting with a combination of firmness and kindness.

I share the story of this particular charter school because in Florida charter schools have now fallen prey to the same testing expectations as the public schools. In Florida, the Florida Comprehensive Assessment Test (FCAT) given in third–tenth grades in reading, third–eight in math, fifth–eight in science, and forth, eight, and tenth in writing.[31] The mission of Alfred Adler Elementary School, which was established under a grant supporting a strong philosophical theory, is being jeopardized because of the infiltration of standardized management and imposed accountability systems. Contemporary educational mandates are clearly not limited to children in public education. In Florida, charter schools are now controlled by mandates against the very principles on which they were given money to establish their schools.

29. Dreikurs et al., *Maintaining Sanity in the Classroom,* 68.
30. DeCosmo, personal communication to author, April 7, 2015.
31. Florida Department of Education, "Florida Department."

When I researched this school, I noticed that its rating on standardized tests was a two out of possible ten by the GreatSchools Rating. GreatSchools—a Florida-based company—utilizes a rating system that advertises categorizing schools to be used as a "simple tool for parents to compare schools based on test scores."[32] When I dug deeper, I found that there are two directors for this organization; the first partner is in a leading technology/software company, and the other partner is a past employee at the U.S. Department of Education under Obama. Also listed as supporters for GreatSchools are the Walton Family Foundation and the Bill and Melinda Gates Foundation. Fascinating strands appear when we have the time to dig below the surface to more deeply explore and question the existence of such school rating systems and the supporting force behind the purpose of the rating. I cannot help but question the motivating factors of an organization, like GreatSchools, that assigns a low test rating to a school that was created on the opposite philosophy of standardized testing and a mandated curriculum. I also question the democratic nature of such rating systems. Instead of allowing for local individuals' voices from and experiences in a given school to be part of the rating, organizations such as GreatSchools have created a quick reference number to decide for us if a school is of "low" or "high" quality. Slowly it seems that students, along with teachers and administrators, are losing their rights for a democratically-rooted education where individuals' voices are heard and trusted.

## THEME SCHOOLS

In 1974, Charlotte-Mecklenburg Schools in North Carolina were federally ordered to desegregate.[33] This prompted the first court ordered bussing in the nation and began the pathway to magnet schools. Today, there are 144,000 students in K-12 that attend one of 164 schools in Charlotte Mecklenburg. Thirty-seven of those

32. Great School Rating, "Alfred Adler Elementary School," para. 5.
33. Brabram, "Swann v. Charlotte-Mecklenburg."

schools are public magnet schools.[34] Because they are public schools, they are federally required to follow the testing requirements dictated by the state, but each one of the nine schools is organized around a different theme. The driving theme of each magnet school then becomes the philosophical focus embedded into the core curriculum. The nine divisions of the magnet schools include: 1) Global Studies Leadership, 2) International Baccalaureate, 3) Language Immersion and World Languages, 4) Learning Immersion and Talent Development, 5) Montessori, Science, Technology, Engineering, Arts and Math, 6) STEM, 7) STEAM, 8) Traditional, and 9) Visual and Performing Arts. The overriding message in the magnet schools emphasizes specialized learning environments that "nurture and enhance students' abilities, aptitudes, interests, and talents."[35]

One school of particular interest is the Collinswood Language Academy, a K-8 magnet school with a nationally recognized dual language program. At Collinswood, the goal of "encouraging their students to grow a high sense of self-esteem and positive cross cultural attitudes"[36] is foremost in their mission. This magnet school believes that dual language learning improves listening, expands both English and Spanish vocabulary, promotes creative thinking, and supports greater career opportunities. Across the board, these students outperform their mono-lingual counterparts on math tests even though math is taught completely in Spanish and the test is given in English. This has prompted a push in North Carolina for dual language education.[37]

At Collinswood Language Academy, a link is drawn between brain research and learning a second language leads to higher-level thinking skills.[38] Through research into the brain, we know the focus for language acquisition opens at birth and tapers off

34. Charlotte-Mecklenburg Schools, "Magnet Programs."
35. Ibid., para. 2.
36. National Association of Magnet, "Magnet Schools of America," para. 4.
37. Maxwell, "Dual-Language Programs Take Root."
38. Thomas and Collier, *Dual Language for a Transformed World.*

in the early teens. Therefore, we should be teaching language well before middle and high school.[39] "Studies show that proficiency in learning a second language depends not on how long non-natives have been speaking the language, but on how early in life they began learning it."[40] The simple fact is that our brains are growing at a faster rate when we are younger. "Children have, on average, 60 percent greater brain activation in the prefrontal cortex than that of adults."[41] The younger we can teach a second language, the higher the probability of a smooth acquisition of dual language.

The safe and nurturing environment with a strong commitment to community are apparent but the most interesting facet of this school is the make-up of its classrooms. In kindergarten, 85 percent of the students' day is spent speaking Spanish and 15 percent English. From first grade on, the day is broken into a 50/50 model of half the day speaking Spanish and the other half of the day is spent speaking English. Reading, writing and science are taught in English and math, social studies, and Spanish literature are taught in Spanish. The composition of the classrooms is divided, 50 percent English speaking and 50 percent Spanish speaking children with the strong philosophy that kids are learning the language from their peers. When I spoke to Nicolette Grant, the Principal of Collinswood Language Academy, she felt that the 50/50 composition of the class makeup and the content presentation of two languages supported positive self-efficacy in the students.[42] This 50/50 classroom composition gave the Spanish speaking kids the opportunity to be a language model for their peers in the Spanish taught classrooms and the English speaking kids the same opportunity to model in the classes presented in English. A sense of pride is developed through kids modeling for their peers.

Along with the peer mentoring, Mrs. Grant felt a great difference in their school was the heavy emphasis on professional development. All teachers are given a survey at the beginning of

39. Sousa, *How the Brain Learns*.
40. Ibid., 183.
41. Jensen, *Enriching the Brain*, 99.
42. Nicolette Grant (principal) in discussion with the author, May 8, 2015.

the year in which they are asked what they want to study and what method of learning would suit them best. These learning style recommendations are then used to create an individual learning plan for the teacher. For example, some teachers are learning through technology like making and sharing Wiki lessons, while some teachers are in a book club where they are reading different books that target their learning interests for that particular year. Meanwhile, other teachers are teaming up to visit classrooms and learn new teaching techniques from each other. The professional development is site-based and ongoing. There is collaborative planning and one of the four yearly required observations must be a teacher-peer observation.

Teachers in Collinswood Language Academy have regular critical conversations about curriculum. Some of these conversations are supported by platforms that are set up in their building to share their thoughts, and some are impromptu in their small groups. There is a school-wide focus to empower teachers. Still, Mrs. Grant expressed the struggle of juggling the local, state, and federal testing and is fully aware of the time that is taken from teaching while testing. Collinswood not only has to meet all of the state required testing but in addition, but they must test all their children in an additional second language test for Spanish. The teachers work regularly brainstorming ways to meet mandated testing constraints while keeping with the philosophy and integrity of their school alive. The success of this school lies in the power of their teachers and their students when they are empowered with the time to communicate.

## NURTURED HEART APPROACH

The Nurtured Heart Approach® (NHA) to education is one of change. Change towards a culture of kindness and compassion—towards becoming the best people we can be. NHA might very well be considered a democratic concept that is embraced by both students and teachers alike. Howard Glasser began as a family psychotherapist, and after many years of trying to change behavior with kids, instead he began to study the relationship dynamics between parents and children. He realized some of the recommendations he was making during his earlier years were actually perpetuating problems, applying energy when things were going wrong versus applying energy when things are going right. In 1997, Glasser developed a simple program that promotes empowerment for children and teachers based on three simple strategies: 1) Absolutely No: Do not energize negative behavior; in other words, calling attention to someone tapping their pencil repeatedly and ignoring when they are sitting there quietly is the opposite of recognizing good behavior; 2) Absolutely Yes: Always see and recognize the positive, for example, when the child is writing or the pencil is down on the desk that is what you recognize; 3) Absolute Clarity: Have clear expectations and boundaries.[43] Students cannot know what to strive for if the expectations are not clear. With the NHA, children learn to understand that they will receive praise and recognition through positive behavior. This supports children building what Glasser calls "Inner Wealth."[44]

Through several email correspondences with Howard Glasser, I was connected with Sarah How, a school psychologist and trainer for the NHA program.[45] When we spoke, Mrs. How was eager to share "whatever we choose to celebrate is what tends to be repeated" and she went on to say "When you change the way you look at things, the things you look at change."[46] What she was referring to was that when we choose to recognize and to celebrate the positive things we see in our classrooms, it has the power to change a school's overall environment. How shared with me a story of a young second grader at West Side Elementary School in North Dakota where she has been conducting training. The young student had "a meltdown" in the hallway. The teacher watched as the young girl pulled herself together, on her own,

---

43. Glasser and Block, *Notching Up the Nurtured Heart Approach*.

44. Childrens Success Foundation, "More About the Nurtured Heart Approach," para. 3.

45. Sarah How, e-mail message to author, April 22, 2015.

46. Ibid.

and regained her composure. As Mrs. How walked by, the teacher shared her pride in this student for her self-composure. At the same time some fifth grade students were at the drinking fountain, and Mrs. How shared this second grader's triumphant battle with self-control. The fifth graders broke into spontaneous clapping for this young student. The pride that the second grade student felt was physically evident. Mrs. How believes the NHA is changing the culture of the entire school.

I spoke to Rose Hardie—the Principal and Special Education Director for Wahpeton Public Schools, North Dakota—who is taking on the challenge of reformation in her district.[47] What began in her building in special education spread to the entire building and is now moving district wide. Wahpeton Public School began the NHA program in 2011. During the initial year of implantation of the program, Mrs. Hardie shared she had 369 office referrals in a building of 150 students. Three years later and as of April of 2015, there had been only forty office referrals. "We were tired of feeling out of control and desperate, we didn't want to feel that way anymore. People are intentional about building inner wealth in children."[48] The change in this school's culture has been incredible.

Professional development has played a major rule in implementing the NHA in the Wahpeton Public Schools and all grants that are currently being written call for training facilitators to become lead learners in the buildings who are moving toward implementation. Mrs. Hardie is adamant that there must be a top-down approach to implement the program successfully. In her experience, if the principal is not on board, the program only works in small pockets, not in the entire building. Moreover, the real support comes from having lead learners trained in the process implementing the NHA and supporting the teachers. Doing this, like any program, is a process that takes time. "In order to create a network within the staff it takes time. It's easy to go down the old neurological pathway to negativity. We have to refuse to

---

47. Rose Hardie (principal and special education director) in discussion with the author, April 29, 2015.

48. Ibid.

go back to that old way and it does take time."⁴⁹ The process took three years to implement and supports a long-term commitment devoted to sustaining this change. The change in the students and the staff is overwhelming, and when reflecting on the experience, Mrs. Hardie stated that "it is a privilege to be part of this change."⁵⁰

Working together to renew education is about changing the culture of our schools over time, and renewal involves literally embracing individual importance, ours and that of our students. Mrs. Hardie shared with me a story about a young, curly-haired, blond Kindergartener who unfortunately contracted a case of head lice. Her parents opted to shave her head rather than go through the expensive and time-consuming process of delousing her hair. When the little girl arrived at school, she shared her "Report for Greatness" (i.e., a weekly individual goal progress report) with her class. She admitted how afraid she was to come to school because of her perceived fear of teasing over her bald head where curls previously existed. She vowed not to cry and to stand up and face her fears. The level of acceptance in the classroom was astonishing. She took control of her fears and proactively headed off any control a bully may have tried to steal from her self-confidence. This story showcases that an NHA is another example of the renewal of democratic education.

Wahpeton schools are in the process of collecting both qualitative and quantitative data to provide the necessary research base to further the drive for this program. They are waiting the results of a recent grant to train eleven more principals in the district. Mrs. Hardie is also in the process of sharing information about this approach in other districts around North Dakota and is currently working on a committee with the Public Department of Instruction to put together a toolbox of programs that work for special education. NHA will be one of the tools recommended for the state.

49. Ibid.
50. Ibid.

## CONCLUSION

There are so many schools that could have been included in this chapter, and the few written about here is only because of limited space. The common link between each of these schools is that they believe in the renewal of education. In different ways, each school embraces renewal in a way that values not only their teachers' contributions but also values the students' individual contributions to the whole of the school. The principals, program creators, and authors that shared their experiences add real-world examples to this chapter. These individuals truly believe that their programs are making a difference by working together to renew their schools because they are seeing and feeling results. They all felt the "bite" that over-testing is causing and each shared the negative effects of standardization on their programs' philosophies. Although these schools are doing an outstanding job of working around the mandates in education today, I cannot help but feel that we need to do more to swing the pendulum of curriculum to a democratic approach for all schools. The final chapter of this book calls for all teachers to take action.

# 7

## A Call for Action

"Committed educators must stand together to fight against the anti-democratic restructuring we are witnessing."[1]

"Those of us working in K-12 public schools and teacher education programs should focus on the immediately local and essentially live the revolution. This would mean, assuming one found the current state of education as unbearable as I have, that one might organize resistance."[2]

Years back, I was privileged to "storm the capital" with my then superintendent and the treasurer. In 1991, the *DeRolph v. State of Ohio*[3] case found funding in Ohio to be inequitable in the over reliance on property taxes; unfortunately, the court never provided a directive as to how to make that happen. One windy

1. Apple, *The Assault on Public Education*, xiii.
2. Taubman, *Teaching by Numbers*, 198.
3. Ohio History Connection, "Ohio History Central."

day in late fall, many educators gathered together in support of prompting our legislature to come up with a plan of action for providing adequate and equitable funding for all of Ohio's public schools. In support of this endeavor, our teachers wrote a song to support changing the funding system in Ohio, and we passed out flyers of the song, held a banner in front of the capital building with many other educators, singing, and protesting peacefully on behalf of our beliefs. Engaging such activism was both frightening and liberating because it was the first time I stood up for a cause with a group of like-minded people. I must say that I have not felt the need to do so since—until now.

I, like Taubman, believe "that our work is to articulate alternatives to the current state of education."[4] Teachers can begin this articulation by reading and empowering themselves through communication with each other, leading to action. I am not here to prescribe what that action will look like, but I do believe that it is time for us to stand together for the democratic right of educating our students in the fashion of excellence; excellence beyond a pre-prescribed definition that outside parties dictate that word to mean.

The actions we take for our students on behalf of their education will affect their learning process, thus affecting their lives and eventually our society as a whole. John Dewey believed that schools were woven into society, not a reflection of society but directly tied into its wellness. I asked Frank X. Ryan— a philosophy professor at Kent State University and a lifelong scholar of John Dewey—his opinion about Dewey's belief in the effects of schools on society. In his response to my question, he shared the following thoughts:

> One of Dewey's most famous quotes, "Education is not preparation for life; education is life itself," sums up what I think you're looking for. Dewey did not believe education should be restricted to imparting knowledge or a specific set of skills that end when one is placed in an assigned social niche, but rather the mastery of a set

---

4. Taubman, *Teaching by Numbers*, 200.

of problem-solving abilities that empower and enfranchise the individual who both contributes to and reaps the benefit of socially constructed goods. As "life itself," education embodies the ideal of "social intelligence"—the ability to effectively diagnose encountered problems and, via democratic action, propose and experimentally achieve concrete solutions he calls the "construction of good."[5]

## ECONOMY, SCHOOLS, AND ACTION

Schools are without a doubt politically influenced. They rely on financial support for survival, both from local taxpayers, as well as state and federal funding for various non-competitive grant programs. Title I funds through the U.S. Department of Education,[6] The Individuals with Disabilities Education Act (IDEA),[7] and various other grants came with mandates that far outweighed the money that was and is handed out for compliance. Unfortunately, the over reliance on these funds to educate all children has become directly tied into compliance with the state and federal laws that now dictate curriculum and content. In other words, schools do not get the state and federal dollars if they do not comply with all the testing regulations and other accompanying mandates.

I believe schools are tied directly into the health and wellbeing of our economy. If this is the case, the mission of educating our youth is of the utmost importance. Let us propose that the mission of education is to guide our students into becoming individuals that contribute their individual aptitudes, talents, and knowledge to the overall betterment of all. Cuban[8] proposes that the mission of public education is "transforming children into civic-minded, independent-thinking, and socially responsible adults committed to both the common good and engaging in productive

---

5. Frank Ryan, personal communication to author, May 15, 2015.
6. U.S. Department of Education, "Laws & Guidance."
7. Individuals with Disabilities Act, "IDEA."
8. Cuban, *Why is it so Hard to Get Good Schools.*

work."[9] Cuban's mission seems somewhat askew from what we see today. Education is more often than not spoken about in terms of global comparison of test scores to further science and industry. Such thinking has the potential for teaching conformity while also ignoring individuality, which is the very basis for the greatness of our country. As highlighted in chapter 6, this ignores and even punishes schools that are trying to follow a mission of democracy as they understand it. Democratic ideas are not acknowledged at the same level as standardized test scores and even charter schools that were given money based on democratic ideas are being forced to uphold standardized goals that mandate the opposite mission for which they were created. If ever there was a time for school renewal and a call to action, it is now.

It is time for teachers to stand together, push back, and fight for the professional freedom to teach in a democratic fashion. One possible venue for this push can be through the existing teachers' union. Recently when I discussed this book with a teacher, she sincerely questioned how teachers should make a change toward a more democratic educational system. I simply said through the union. She immediately got defensive and replied, "But we aren't against our school or our principals, we are all just trying to do the best we can with the situation." There seemed to be a perception with this teacher that the union is only local, taking care of local pay and fringes. However, that is not the only mission of our teachers' union. For example, the American Federation of Teachers[10] proudly displays their mission statement:

> The American Federation of Teachers is a union of professionals that champions fairness; democracy; economic opportunity; and high-quality public education, healthcare and public services for our students, their families and our communities. We are committed to advancing these principles through community engagement,

---

9. Ibid., 6.

10. American Federation of Teachers, "AFT a Union of Professionals," para. 1.

organizing, collective bargaining and political activism, and especially through the work our members do.

I see none of the democratic principles that are written in this mission statement actually being supported through any advocacy or action toward these goals. Collective, local, and consorted effort to remind the union of their responsibility plainly stated in their mission would be a bold move in the right direction.

Finland's teachers worked through their teachers' union to prompt national change. Finland is one nation that knows firsthand how the economy is directly tied into public education and decided, as a society, to change. And it might be said that their change was characterized as a time "that challenged conventional beliefs, searched for innovation, and increased trust in schools and their abilities to find the best ways to raise the quality of student learning."[11] In the mid-1950's, many Finnish civic organizations pushed for a new comprehensive school system. As part of that effort, the Finnish Primary School Teachers' Association (FPSTA) published a detailed educational development program that took five years in the making. This publication "stimulated a national discussion that clearly focused the need to enhance equality and social justice in Finnish society through a more equitable education system."[12] New legislation was procured, and Finland is now an exemplar example of change and educational success.

> With its unexpectedly and consistently superlative performance on international tests of student achievement, its possession of the narrowest achievement gaps in the world, and its equally high rankings on ratings of economic competitiveness, corporate transparency, and general well-being and quality of life, this little Nordic country of barely 5.5 million people has illuminated a different path to educational and economic goals than those being forged by the Anglo-American groups of nations.[13]

11. Sahlberg, *Finnish Lessons*, 35.
12. Ibid., 20.
13. Ibid., xviii.

OUT OF THE DARK

There are some important factors that Salhberg highlights that were important objectives during this initiative and stand today. Finland limits testing and values responsibility and trust, while leaving the leadership responsibilities to the educational professionals. They know that you must compensate professionals for their dedication, continued research and continued commitment to staying current in an ever-changing field. In order to support professionals in the changing field of education, a great deal of money was and is spent on staff development that encourages critical reflections and exploration around important curricular and pedagogical themes. Questions such as: "What is knowledge?," "How do pupils learn?," and "How do schools change?"[14] have the expectation of supporting children as they change and grow individually, as they become more advanced academically, and as they mature into their role as adults in a changing society. Finnish teachers banded together and took on the responsibility for curriculum development. The responsibility was entrusted to them, and it changed their nation.

## DEMOCRACY: A DIRECTION FOR CURRICULUM DEVELOPMENT

Has the time come for those of us in the field of education in the United States to develop curriculum that is aligned with our mission for educating children? Cuban[15] shares that, according to opinion polls and surveys, people agree on the main mission of education our youth.

> Both progressives and traditionalists want students to put into practice the knowledge they gain, display in their behavior the moral attitudes they learn, and use skills acquired in school. Both progressives and traditionalists respond to differences in students' interests, motivation, talents, and backgrounds. Both want their children to become literate, self-disciplined, self-reliant

14. Ibid., 34.
15. Cuban, *Why is it so Hard to Get Good Schools.*

adults engaged in productive work, and committed to sustaining democratic practices in their communities and nation.[16]

The most important impact that will shape education is deciding what the mission of education should be, developing curriculum around that purpose, and deeply embodying that said and lived mission. We could ask ourselves if we are presently preparing our children for a stagnant, predictable world that is anything but stagnant and predictable. Change is the only constant in our world; when we search for something that is deeper like a more meaningful, fulfilling education, we "find more deeply held beliefs and assumptions that also exert powerful influence on our actions."[17] Engaging in this type of learning, we change and so does our society. Are we, as citizens of the United States, satisfied that our country is functioning as a democratic society? I believe change is needed for our schools and for our society. As teachers and as citizens, I believe it is time to take a strong look at ourselves, and we must start engaging in honest critical dialogue about doing our part in changing our country through ourselves and our students. This challenge begins by developing a democratic curriculum direction and then striving to live through that moral path.

We have examples of schools and brave pioneers who spent their lifetimes trying to build schools that experimented with democracy such as John Dewey in his Laboratory School,[18] Jane Adams and her Hull House,[19] and the countless other present-day schools some of which have been mentioned and used as illustrations in this book's prior chapters. Unfortunately, we cannot seem to duplicate these experiments on a larger scale across our nation for all students. Experimental schools seem to get trapped in the theories and ideals only to be lost in the experiment; that is, they somehow become mired and stagnated in the inability to spark similar action into other schools. There are, however, small pockets

16. Ibid., 35.
17. Caine and Caine, *Education of the Edge,* 85.
18. Mayhew and Edwards, *Laboratory School of the University of Chicago.*
19. Hendry, *Engendering Curriculum History.*

of teachers bravely trying to take on curriculum development in their own classrooms. These are teachers who have been engaged in the democratic challenge for some time. The push, within this book and in many of the authors referenced here, is for more and more of these democratically empowered educators to share and grow in their own professional knowledge of what they know to be the best education for their students. For us to show that educating differently is possible and to ignite, invite, and inspire others to join the call for change. This requires redefining teachers as leaders which in research is supported as an essential element in a healthy school.[20]

## TEACHER LEADERS

One example of cultivating and supporting teachers as lead learners is taking place in the state of Ohio. In 2009, a grant was submitted by Kent State University (KSU) to the Ohio Department of Education to be one of five states to begin a Teacher Leader Endorsement Program (TLEP).[21] The Ohio Board of Regents (OBR) officially sanctioned KSU's TLEP through this grant to incorporate a deeper understanding of collegial reflective inquiry through subject understandings that are integrated with democratic self and social understandings.[22] KSU's TLEP with its democratically-rooted program acknowledges that there are many possible scenarios for teachers to utilize their leadership potential. One particular research strand was apparent as a result of this grant, the initiative has to be supported by administrators or the program does not spread beyond the individual teacher leaders.[23]

In 2015, an additional large grant was received from the Ohio Department of Education for KSU to support additional districts in developing teachers as leaders, empowered to embark upon

20. Barth, "Teacher Leader." Smylie et al., "Exploring New Approaches to Teacher Leadership."
21. Ohio Department of Education, "Teacher Leader Endorsement"
22. Henderson and Gornik, *Transformative Curriculum Leadership*.
23. Samford, "Exploring Sustained Change."

their own democratic curriculum-based journey of understanding. For the purposes of this grant, teacher leaders are defined as "committed to work as democratic visionaries, colleagues, and pedagogical artists through disciplined study and practice, and they embrace the personal journeys of becoming/embodying that this work entails."[24] Currently, two schools, one urban school and one suburban school are participating in promoting and supporting teacher leadership in their district. As part of this initiative, all administrators (both central office and building) will work to create a platform to support the teacher leaders when they return to the district and the building.

Slowly, teachers are beginning to talk; small pockets of individuals are taking on the challenge of leading other teachers, learning as they move forward in action for developing democratic curriculum to support their journey and that of their students. One such teacher took part in KSU's original TLEP grant cohort. She shared her story with me, and I am sharing her reflections with you here.

> *It has been four years since I completed my work with the Teacher Leader Cadre at KSU, four years since I was introduced to the idea of teaching for 3S understanding. These have been my strongest years as a classroom teacher: I see my role as an educator as someone who is a coach and mentor to my students in their learning. This is a role that has evolved as a result of using 3S understanding to inform my teaching. Instead of being the captain who pilots the ship (taking eager travelers as well as unwitting and unwilling passengers to a far-off destination) or a band director (selecting the repertoire and controlling the pace, pitch, and performance of the musicians), my role in the classroom has changed to that of a coach: someone who gets to know the players, helps them to understand their talents as well as skills needed for the game, and then stands back and provides guidance as they play the game for themselves. I am a stronger teacher, more responsive*

---

24. James Henderson, personal communication to author, October 26, 2015.

to the individual talents and needs of my students, and I believe that this is a result of approaching my teaching with 3S understanding at the basis. Even though I may have a class roster of 28 students, when I plan with the idea of connecting subject matter understanding with democratic self and social understanding, I have a much greater sense of reaching students one-to-one. I have developed classroom activities and assignments which give students choice and ask them to reflect about their learning and what it means in the world.

In one sense, I have less "control" than I used to, but classroom discussions are richer, written reflections are more authentic representations of individual inquiry, and students come to class eager to participate in the work of reading, talking, and writing about literature and its connections to them and their society. I have come to understand that the great value of the study of writing and of literature is that it creates the very capacity for empathy that is needed for democratic self and social understanding. While the last four years has certainly seen the growth of Common Core requirements in our state and my district, I have not found this to be a barrier to teaching for 3S understanding. To some extent, the Common Core emphasis on non-fiction texts and reading a text multiple times for deeper understanding complements 3S thinking. For example, as my students and I were working out way through Hemingway's A Farewell to Arms last spring, we were of course interested in the plot, character development, and symbolic elements of the novel. However, there were many elements of the novel which students could connect to their own lives and our changing times. The alienation of the Lost Generation, illustrated by the thoughts and actions Frederick Henry and Catherine, inspired my 21st century students to consider the many ways that modernist ideas have shaped their own lives and events in our world today. Their journals reflected their own confusion in a world where texting, Facebook, Snapchat, and Twitter have the power to connect individuals and at the same time make individuals feel even more isolated. Class discussions connected the experiences of World War I to those in modern-day in Afghanistan, Serbia, and Darfur; students

## A Call for Action

contemplated not only the response but the responsibilities of the individual to the course of history and the greater good of society. An understanding of 3S understanding enriches the possibilities of teaching the Common Core.

In the first paragraph of this reflection, I said that becoming a Teacher Leader has enriched my classroom teaching. It has. However, one area that has been a disappointment to me has been my (in)ability to affect change as a Teacher Leader among my peers. Despite my years of teaching experience, despite my training in 3S understanding, despite my achievement of a Teacher Leader Endorsement addition to my teaching license, my desire to be a "teacher leader" in my district is certainly underutilized and largely ignored by administrators and fellow teachers. Oh, I am involved in many leadership roles in my district: I am "Collegial Coach" (essentially Department Chair) of the high school Language Arts department; I serve on the district LPDC committee; I am a member of the Building Leadership Team; I serve on the committee which plans the high school master schedule each year; I mentor university students who are in the observation phase and the student teaching phase of their teacher preparation. However, all of these were things I did before going through Teacher Leader training.

There is, in my district, no place for someone with Teacher Leader credentials, nor is there any incentive or encouragement for any of my colleagues to become a Teacher Leader. I am approaching the time when I must write my application for renewal of my Master Teacher status with the State of Ohio, and I am still the only person in my building and my district who is a Master Teacher. When I encourage my friends and colleagues to pursue Master Teacher or Teacher Leader status, they say, "Why should I? What does it mean?" And those are very good questions for which my district has no answer. When I spoke with our district curriculum director about encouraging others to pursue Master Teacher credentials — after he sent me to a Master Teacher meeting in Columbus last year — he ignored me. Perhaps that is not fair — he does have many important issues to deal with, such as the Third Grade Reading Guarantee, Common Core, and PARCC testing. However, he has never responded to the issue in conversation or in email communications. Our Superintendent is proud of my credentials: whenever we are at community meetings or county professional development sessions, he introduces me as a "Master Teacher" and "Teacher Leader" in our district. Yet, when I spoke to him about providing some incentive for others to join me, he said, "That is something our administration would support if the union proposed it in our next contract negotiations." Well, that's good to know, but I am only one out of 130 teachers in my district. I can — and I plan to — take a leadership role in introducing and advocating the issue for our negotiating team. However, as the negotiations team selects the 5–7 top issues which affect the greatest number of teachers in the district, it will be a hard sell to convince them that defining responsibilities or encouraging compensation for teacher leaders is of importance: my argument, although valid, runs the risk of appearing selfish and self-serving since, at the moment, it would appear to be an issue only for me.

 I do utilize my Teacher Leader training all of the time with my colleagues. As Collegial Coach, it is my responsibility to foster communication and collaboration among members of my department. I take every opportunity to encourage the other English teachers to work together, especially in this time of curricular change due to Common Core. I do not think I have been terribly successful. Collaboration, at this point, tends to be a simple sharing of handouts; for example, one English 12 teacher does the lesson plans and prepares class materials for everyone teaching the course. I worked with our football coach/English 11 teacher to create an "English student rubric" to help students self-assess and help teachers have a better understanding of student interests, study habits, and learning styles. It's a great rubric, but I think I am the only one who uses it. Our "collaborative" curriculum writing, made necessary with implementation of the Common Core, ended up as a draft written by one person — me (because I had a student teacher that semester) — which was then reviewed and approved by department members. I made every attempt to work with suggestions and ideas from members of the Language Arts team. I listened carefully to comments from my department members and worked with every idea they suggested so they would feel part of the curriculum development process, so that they would feel ownership of the curriculum. We have changed book titles in the curriculum to ones they would rather teach, finding materials and suggesting approaches to the new text which are in line with Common Core. I continue to do everything I can to foster a collaborative and sharing environment for our department, so I find it very discouraging to know that they are not actually teaching the curriculum: although they approved it, because they didn't truly collaborate in its creation, they take no ownership for it. I have spoken to the building principal — who is responsible for their evaluations — and to the curriculum director, asking for assistance in getting those in my department to actually teach the curriculum which is written for the courses they teach. Both principal and curriculum director nod and agree that it is important to teach the curriculum. The curriculum director went so far as to attend a department meeting and explicitly say to the group that they must follow our curriculum as it is written. But comments made to a whole group are often ignored by the individuals who need improvement.

 I met with the principal on several occasions to elicit guidance on how to handle the situation of an Honors English teacher who assigned no writing assignments, about whom there were many parent complaints. The principal and I strategized ways to work with this individual over the course of a year, some actions to be taken by me, and some by the principal through the formal observation and evaluation process. Yet, at the end of the year, when I met with this individual to inform him that he would no longer be teaching Honors English because there had been no improvement, I discovered that the "courageous conversations" which the principal had said he would have as part of the evaluation process had never happened. It was extremely awkward: I found myself having to say things which only a supervisor should say to an employee, and I found myself having to say "I don't know" when this teacher asked me why the principal had never said any *of these things to him. I felt that the principal and I were collaborating in helping a teacher to improve. I discovered that the principal's support was nominal; I discovered that without true administrative support, there is nothing I can do to accomplish change in my department or in my building. I can try to inspire others by my actions, but I can't make them become more effective teachers. That change must come from within.*

*There are still opportunities to use my Teacher Leader inclinations and abilities. I have developed some rather close relationships with others in the building who are NOT in my department, sharing ideas about evaluating writing (for non-English teachers), learning about "flipping" technology which can enhance student learning. I have also developed relationships with teachers from around the country whom I have met by attending state-wide and national conferences. I can participate in regularly scheduled Twitter chats (Flipping on Monday evenings, Edmodo on Wednesdays, AP on Thursdays . . . ) and collaborate with teachers who desire support for what they do in the classroom. I can follow the AP English Literature blog, getting ideas and sharing ideas to make my class more rich. I am inspired when I get to know teachers who "co-teach" with someone who lives in a different state, accomplishing this through daily Skype sessions for planning, assessment, and sharing of ideas. These teachers, like me, find that it is very difficult to be collaborative with members of their own department, in their own buildings and districts, and so they join a network of teachers around the world. There is enormous potential and enormous support for this activity online. I just wish there was there was equal potential and support for the Teacher Leader in my own building and district.*[25]

The triumph, along with the exhaustion of this teacher is evident in her writing. Through teachers banding together, change toward a more democratic educational system might finally be birthed from within the United States. We must take an active role

25. Anonymous Teacher Leader, email message to author, February 20, 2015.

## A Call for Action

in the future of education. We must not allow ourselves to stand in the shadows any longer. We must work together to be living examples of democracy for our students. We must pull together as professionals in our field and refuse to be neutral. Arm yourself with information. Take offense at the standardization requirements you are being forced to implement on a regular basis. Think about the affects of standardization on this generation's ability to create, originate, formulate and design ideas for the future.

My hope is that this book has begun to lay out a direction for change in the current state of educational affairs in the United States. And my prayer is that we have the courage to make it happen.

# Bibliography

American Federation of Teachers. "Mission." Accessed July 9, 2015. www.aft.org/about/mission.

Apple, Michael W. *Ideology and Curriculum*. 3rd ed. New York: Routledge, 2004.

———. "Foreword." In *The Assault on Public Education*, edited by William H. Watkins, ix–xiv. New York: Teachers College Press, 2012.

Armstrong, Thomas. *The Best Schools: How Human Development Research Should Inform Educational Practice*. Alexandria: Association for Supervision and Curriculum Development, 2006.

Ball, Stephen J. "The Teacher's Soul and the Terrors of Performativity." *Journal of Educational Policy 18* (2003) 215–28.

Barth, Ronald S. "Teacher leader." *Phi Delta Kappan, 82* (2001) 443–40.

———. "Foreword." In *How Leaders Learn: Cultivating Capacities for School Improvement,* by Gordon A. Donaldson, ix–xi. New York: Teachers College Press, 2008.

Bell, Brenda, John Gaventa, and John Peters, eds. *We Make the Road by Walking: Conversations on Education and Social Change Myles Horton and Paulo Freire*. Philadelphia: Temple University Press, 1990.

Bobbitt, Franklin. "Scientific Method in Curriculum-Making." In *The Curriculum Studies Reader*. 2nd ed., edited by David J. Flinders and Stephen J. Thornton, 2–16. New York: Routledge, 2004.

———. *The Curriculum*. Boston: Houghton Mifflin, 1918.

Brabram, Robin. *Swann v. Charlotte-Mecklenburg Board of Education*. Last modified January 1, 2006. NCpedia.org/Swann-v-charlotte-mecklenburg-board.

Brookfield, Stephen D. *Becoming a Critically Reflective Teacher*. San Francisco: Jossey-Bass, 1995.

Buckingham, Marcus, and Curt Coffman. *First, Break all the Rules*. New York: Simon & Schuster, 1999.

Burbank, Mary D., and Don Kauchak. "An Alternative Model for Professional Development: Investigations into Effective Collaboration." *Teaching and Teacher Education 19* (2003) 499–514.

# Bibliography

Caine, Renate N., and Geoffrey Caine. *Education on the Edge of Possibility.* Alexandria: Association for Supervision and Curriculum Development, 1997.

Carothers, Wendy L. *Qualitative Mini-study: Inclusion or Co-teaching?* Unpublished manuscript, 2007.

Charlotte-Mecklenburg Schools. *Magnet Programs: 2015–2016 School Options Guide.* Accessed May 20, 2015. www.cms.k12.nc.us/cmsdepartments/ci/MagnetPrograms/Pages/default.aspx.

Children's Success Foundation. *More About the Nurtured Heart Approach.* Last modified 2015. www.childrenssuccessfoundation.com/about-nurtured-heart-approach/more-about-the-nurtured-heart-approach.

Clement, Mieke, and Roland Vandenberghe. "Teachers' Professional Development: A Solitary or Collegial Adventure." *Teaching and Teacher Education 16* (2000) 81–101.

Cochran-Smith, Marilyn. "The Unforgiving Complexity of Teaching, Avoiding Simplicity in the Age of Accountability." *Journal of Teacher Education 54* (2003) 3–5.

Collins, Jim. *Good to Great.* New York: Harper Collins, 2001.

Common Core State Standards Initiative. *Standards in your State.* Last modified 2016. www.corestandards.org/standards-in-your-state/.

Conley, Sharon, and Naftaly Glasman. "Fear, the School Organization and Teacher Evaluation." *Educational Policy 22* (2008) 63–85.

Cuban, Larry. *Why Is It So Hard to Get Good Schools?* New York: Teachers College Press, 2003.

Darley, John, M., and C. Daniel Batson. "From Jerusalem to Jericho: A Study of Situational and Dispositional Variables in Helping Behavior." *Journal of Personality and Social Psychology 27* (1973) 100–08.

DeSteno, David. *The Truth About Trust: How it Determines Success in Life, Love, Learning, and More.* New York: Penguin, 2014.

Dewey, John. "Creative Democracy: The Task Before Us." In *The Essential Dewey: The Later Works. 1929–1953*, vol. 14, edited by Larry A. Hickman, and Thomas M. Alexander, 340–43. Bloomington: Indiana University Press, 1988.

———. "Democracy is Radical." In *The Essential Dewey: The Later Works, 1925–1953*, vol. 11, edited by Larry A. Hickman, and Thomas M. Alexander, 337–39. Bloomington: Indiana University Press, 1988.

———. *Experience & Education.* New York: Touchstone, 1938.

———. "Nationalizing Education." In *The Essential Dewey: The Middle Works 1899–1924*, vol. 10, edited by Larry A. Hickman, and Thomas M. Alexander, 265–29. Bloomington: Indiana University Press, 1988.

———. "My Pedagogic Creed." In *The Curriculum Studies Reader.* 2nd ed., edited by David. J. Flinders and Stephen J. Thornton, 17–23. New York: Routledge, 2004.

Dewey, John, and Arthur F. Bentley, *Knowing and the Known.* Boston: The Beacon, 1949.

# BIBLIOGRAPHY

Donaldson, Gordon A. *How Leaders Learn: Cultivating Capacities for School Improvement*. New York: Teachers College Press, 2008.

Donaldson, Morgaen L., and Susan Moore Johnson. "FTA Teachers How Long Do They Teach? Why Do They Leave?" *Phi Delta Kappan International* October 4, 2011. http://www.edweek.org/ew/articles/2011/10/04/kappan_donaldson.html.

Dreikurs, Rudolf, Bernice Bronia Grunwald., and Floy C. Pepper. *Maintaining Sanity in the Classroom: Classroom Management Techniques*. 2nd ed. New York: Taylor & Francis, 1998.

DuFour, Richard. "What is a 'Professional Learning Community'?" *Educational Leadership 61* (2004) 6–11.

———. "In the Right Context." *The Principal* (Winter 2001) 14–7.

Dweck, Carol S. *Mindset: The New Psychology of Success*. New York: Ballantine, 2008.

Dwornik, Isabel Ann. "A Comparison of Educational Theory: Alfred Adler & John Dewey." *The Journal of Individual Psychology 59* (2003) 52–71.

Earl, Lorna. "Accountability as a Collective Professional Responsibility." In *Leading Educational Change: Global Issues, Challenges, and Lessons on Whole-System Reform*, edited by Helen J. Malone, 101–06. New York: Teachers College Press, 2013.

Education Commission of the States. *Teaching at Risk: A Call to Action*. Accessed February 11, 2016. http://www.ctl.vcu.edu/media/ctl/documents/TeachingAtRisk.pdf.

Edwards, Thomas G., and Sarah M. Hensien. "Changing Instructional Practice Through Action Research." *Journal of Mathematics Teacher Education 2* (1999) 187.

Eisner, Elliot W. *The Kind of School We Need: Personal Essays*. Portsmouth: Heinemann, 1998.

———. "Educational Objectives—Help or Hindrance?" In *The Curriculum Studies Reader*. 2nd ed., edited by David J. Flinders and Stephen J. Thornton, 85–91. New York: Routledge, 2004.

Elbow, Peter. *Embracing Contraries: Explorations in Learning and Teaching*. New York: Oxford University Press, 1986.

Engstrom, Mary E., and Lana M. Danielson. "Teachers' Perceptions of an On-Site Staff Development Model." *Clearing House 79* (2006) 170–73.

Feiman-Nemser, Sharon. "From Preparation to Practice: Designing a Continuum to Strengthen and Sustain Teaching." *Teachers College Record 103* (2001) 1013–55.

Filho, Walter Leal. "Teaching Sustainable Development at University Level: Current Trends." *Journal of Baltic Science Education 9* (2010) 273–84.

Fisher, Roger, William Ury, and Bruce Patton. *Getting to Yes: Negotiating Agreement Without Giving In*. New York: Penguin, 2011.

Fishman, Christine K. "Sowing Holistic Understanding: Building a Disciplinary Community." In *Reconceptualizing Curriculum Development: Inspiring*

*and Informing Action*, by James G. Henderson et al., 68–84. New York: Routledge, 2015.
Fliegel, Seymour, and James MacGuire. *Miracle in East Harlem: The Fight for Choice in Public Education*. New York: Three Rivers, 1994.
Flinders, David J., and Stephen J. Thornton, eds. *The Curriculum Studies Reader*. 2nd ed. New York: Routledge, 2004.
Florida Department of Education. *Florida Department of Education*. Accessed June 3, 2015. fl/doe.org/contact-us/search.stml?q=tested+grades.
Foshay, Arthur W. "Scientific Inquiry: Explanations and Limits." In *Forms of Curriculum Inquiry*, edited by Edward C. Short, 89–99. Albany: State University of New York Press, 1991.
Freire, Paulo. "Pedagogy of the Oppressed." In *The Curriculum Studies Reader*. 2nd ed., edited by David J. Flinders and Stephen J. Thornton, 125–33. New York: Routledge, 2004.
———. *Pedagogy of the Oppressed*. New York: Continuum, 1997.
———. *Teachers as Cultural Workers, Letters to Those Who Dare Teach*. Boulder: Westview, 1998.
Fullan, Michael. "Foreword." In *Leading Educational Change: Global Issues, Challenges, and Lessons on Whole-system Reform*, edited by H. J. Malone, xi–xii. New York: Teachers College Press, 2013.
———. *The New Meaning of Educational Change*. 4th ed. New York: Teachers College Press, 2007.
———. *What's Worth Fighting for in the Principalship*. 2nd ed. New York: Teachers College Press, 2008.
Gamble, Charles W., and Edward C. Watkins Jr. "Combining the Child Discipline Approaches of Alfred Adler & William Glasser: A Case Study." *The Journal of Adlerian Theory, Research & Practice* 39 (1983) 156–64.
Gardner, Howard. *Frames of Mind*. 3rd ed. New York: Basic Books, Perseus, 1993.
Gerson, Jack. "The Neoliberal Agenda and the Response of Teachers Unions." In *The Assault on Public Education: Confronting the Politics of Corporate School Reform*, edited by William H. Watkins, 97–124. New York: Teachers College Press, 2012.
Glasser, William. *Choice Theory in the Classroom*. New York: HarperCollins, 1988.
Glasser, William, and Melissa Lynn Block. *Notching Up the Nurtured Heart Approach: The New Inner Wealth Initiative for Educators*. Tucson: Center for the Difficult Child, 2012.
Goleman, Daniel. *Emotional Intelligence: Why it Can Matter More Than IQ*. New York: Bantam Dell, 1995.
Gomez, Mary Louise, Rebecca W. Black, and Anna-Ruth Allen. "'Becoming' a Teacher." *Teachers College Record* 109 (2007) 2109–35.
GreatSchools Rating. *Alfred Adler Elementary School*. Last modified August 30, 2015. www.greatschools.org.

# Bibliography

Greene, Maxine. *The Dialectic of Freedom.* New York, NY: Teachers College, 1988.

——. *Releasing the Imagination: Essays on Education, the Arts and Social Change.* San Francisco: Jossey-Bass, 1995.

Griest, Jen, Jennifer L. Schneider, Susan School, and Konni Stagliano. "Lead learning stories: A narrative montage." In *Reconceptualizing Curriculum Development: Inspiring and Informing Action,* by James G. Henderson et al., 139–168. New York: Routledge, 2015.

Guskey, Thomas R. "Professional Development and Teacher Change." *Teachers and Teaching; Theory and Practice 8* (2002) 381–91.

——. "Staff Development and Teacher Change." *Educational Leadership* 57–60, 1985.

——. "What Makes Professional Development Effective?" *Phi Delta Kappan 84* (2003) 748–50. doi: 10.1177/003172170308401007

Hackney, Catherine, and James G. Henderson. "Develop the Instructional Leadership Capacity of Staff." In *The New Instructional Leadership: ISLLC Standard Two,* edited by Rose Ylimaki, 107–123. New York: Taylor & Francis, 2013.

Hargrove, Tracy, Bradford L. Walker, Richard A. Huber, Stephanie Z. Corrigan, and Christopher Moore. "No teachers Left Behind: Supporting Teachers as They Implement Standards-based Reform in a Test-Based Education Environment." *Education. 124* (2004) 567–72.

Henderson, James G. "Collegial Reflective Inquiry: A Study & Practice Agenda." Lecture at Kent State University, Kent, OH, April 2, 2012.

——. "Curriculum Discourse and the Question of Empowerment." *Theory into Practice XXXI* (3), 204–9, 1992.

——. "Teacher Leadership in Democratic Societies: A Curriculum Study Approach." Presentation at Kent State University, Kent, OH, April 7, 2012.

Henderson, James G., et al. *Reconceptualizing Curriculum Development: Inspiring and Informing Action.* New York: Routledge, 2015.

Henderson, James G., and Rosemary Gornik. *Transformative Curriculum Leadership.* 3rd ed. Upper Saddle River: Pearson Education, 2007.

Hendry, Petra Munroe. *Engendering Curriculum History.* New York: Routledge, 2011.

Hoover, Randy. "Understanding the Basic Problems with the Use of Value Added in Ohio." *The Teacher Advocate,* 2014a. teacher-advocate.com/content/understanding-basic-problems-use-value-added-ohio.

——. "PARCC & Common Core." *The Teacher Advocate.* 2014b. Teacher-advocate.com/content/parcc-common-core.

——. "Understanding the Difference Between Authentic Accountability and Pseudo Accountability." *The Teacher Advocate.* 2014c. Teacher-advocate.com/content/understanding-difference-between-authentic-accountability-and-pseudo-accountability.

## BIBLIOGRAPHY

Horton, Myles, and Paulo Freire. In *We Make the Road by Walking: Conversations on Education and Social Change,* edited by Brenda Bell, John Gaventa, and John Peters. Philadelphia: Temple University Press, 1990.

Howard, Adam, and Bruce Parker. "Resisting silence." *Democracy & Education 18* (2009) 18–25.

Individuals with Disabilities Education Act. *The Library of Congress Thomas,* Accessed May 6, 2015. http://thomas.loc.gov/home/thomas.php.

Ingersoll, Richard M. "The teacher shortage: A Case of Wrong Diagnosis and Wrong Prescription." *NASSP Bulletin 86* (2002) 16–31.

Jacobs, Heidi Hayes. *Curriculum 21, Essential Education for a Changing World.* Alexandria: Association for Supervision and Curriculum Development, 2010.

Jensen, Eric. *Enriching the Brain: How to Maximize Every Learner's Potential.* San Francisco: Jossey-Bass, 2006.

Kegan, Robert. *The Evolving Self: Problem and Process in Human Development.* Cambridge: Harvard University Press, 1982.

———. *In Over Our Heads: The Mental Demands of Modern Life.* Cambridge: Harvard University Press, 1994.

Kegan, Robert, and Lisa Laskow-Lahey. *Immunity to Change: How to Overcome it and Unlock the Potential in Yourself and Your Organization.* Boston: Harvard Business School Publishing, 2009.

Kincheloe, Joe L., and Peter McLaren. Rethinking Critical Theory and Qualitative Research. In *The Sage Handbook of Qualitative Research.* 3rd ed., edited by Norman K. Denzin and Yvonna S. Lincoln, 303–42. Thousand Oaks: SAGE, 2005.

King, M. Bruce, and Fred M. Newmann. "Building School Capacity Through Professional Development: Conceptual and Empirical Considerations." *The International Journal of Educational Management 15* (2001) 86–93.

Kliebard, Herbert M. "The Rise of Scientific Curriculum-Making and its Aftermath." In *The Curriculum Studies Reader.* 2nd ed., edited by David J. Flinders and Stephen J. Thornton, 38–50. New York: Routledge, 2004.

———. *The Struggle for the American Curriculum.* 3rd ed. New York: Routledge, 2004.

Kopkowski, Cynthia. "Why They Leave." *National Education Association Today Magazine,* April 5, 2008. http://www.nea.org/home/12630.htm.

Kopp, W. *Teach for America Annual Letter.* Accessed May 10, 2015. http://www.teachforamerica.org/.

Leithwood, Kenneth, Karen Seashore Louis, Stephen Anderson, and Kyla Wahlstrom. "How Leadership Influences Student Learning: A Research Review." *Center for Applied Research and Educational Improvement and Ontario Institute for Studies in Education,* October, 2004. http://www.wallacefoundation.org/knowledge-center/school-leadership/key-research/Pages/How-Leadership-Influences-Student-Learning.aspx.

Lewin, Kurt. *Resolving Social Conflicts: Field Theory in Social Science.* Washington: American Psychological Association, 1997.

# Bibliography

Lipman, Pauline. "Neoliberal Urbanism, Race, and Urban School Reform." In *The Assault on Public Education: Confronting the Politics of Corporate School Reform*, edited by William H. Watkins, 33–54. New York: Teachers College Press, 2012.

Lovett, Susan, and Alison Gilmore. "Teachers' Learning Journeys: The Quality Learning Circle as a Model of Professional Development." *School Effectiveness and School Improvement 14* (2003) 189–211.

Lumpe, Andrew T. "Research-based Professional Development: Teachers Engaged in Professional Learning Communities." *Journal of Science Teacher Education 18* (2007) 125–28.

Maslow, Abraham. "A Theory of Human Motivation." *Psychological Review 50*, 1943.

Maxwell, Lesli A. "Dual-language Programs Take Root in N.C." *Education Week 34* (2014) 14–5.

Mayhew, Katherine Camp, and Anna Camp Edwards. *The Laboratory School of the University of Chicago (1896–1903)*. Atherton: Atherton, 1965.

Merriam-Webster Dictionary Online, s.v. "collegiality." Accessed February 24, 2015. http://www.merriam-webster.com/dictionary/collegiality.

———. s.v. "cooperative." Accessed February 24, 2015. http://www.merriam-webster.com/dictionary/cooperative.

———. s.v. "standards." Accessed November 17, 2014. http://www.merriam-webster.com/dictionary/standards.

———. s.v. "standardize." Accessed November 17, 2014. http://www.merriam-webster.com/dictionary/standardize.

McDonald, Angus S. "The Prevalence and Effects of Test Anxiety in School Children." *Educational Psychology 21* (2010) 89–101.

McGuffey, William Holmes. *McGuffey's Eclectic Primer*. Cincinnati: Truman & Smith, 1836.

Meier, Deborah. *The Power of Their Ideas: Lessons for America from a Small School in Harlem*. 2nd ed. Boston: Beacon, 2002a.

———. *In Schools We Trust: Creating Communities of Learning in an Era of Testing and Standardization*. Boston: Beacon, 2002b.

Mischel, Walter. *The Marshmallow Test: Mastering Self-Control*. New York: Hachette Book, 2014.

Nancy, Jean-Luc. *The Truth of Democracy*. Translated by Pascale-Anne Brault and Michael Naas. Bronx: Fordham University Press, 2010.

National Archives. *The Declaration of Independence*. Accessed December 3, 2014. http://www.archives.gov/exhibits/charters/declaration_transcript.html.

National Association of Magnet in America. "Success Story: Celebrating World Cultures and Embracing Diversity Through Two Languages." Last modified 2013. http://www.magnet.edu/news-and-action/success-stories/collinswood.

# BIBLIOGRAPHY

National Center for Research on Evaluation, Standards, and Student Testing. *Standards for Educational Accountability Systems.* Los Angeles: UCLA, 2002.

Null, Wesley. *Curriculum: From Theory to Practice.* Lanham: Rowman & Littlefield, 2011.

Ohio Department of Education. *Academic Content Standards Extended.* Last modified July 21, 2015. http://education.ohio.gov/Topics/Special-Education/Students-With-Disabilities-1.

———. *Value-Added Student Growth Measure.* Last modified December 22, 2015. http://education.ohio.gov/Topics/Teaching/Educator-Evaluation-System/Ohio-s-Teacher-Evaluation-System/Student-Growth-Measures/Value-Added-Student-Growth-Measure.

Ohio Department of Education, and Ohio Board of Regents. *Teacher Leader Endorsement Ohio Program Standards.* Accessed May 9, 2015. http://education.ohio.gov/.

Ohio History Connection. *Ohio History Central: DeRolph v. State of Ohio.* Accessed December 5, 2014. www.ohiohistorycentral.org/w/DeRolph_v._State_of_Ohio.

Palmer, Joy A., ed. *Fifty Modern Thinkers on Education.* New York: Routledge, 2001.

Perrone, Vito. "Reflections on Teaching: Learning to Teach and Teaching to Learn." *Teachers College Record* 98 (1997) 637–52.

Pignatelli, Frank. "Everyday Courage in the Midst of Standardization in Schools." *Schools: Studies in Education* 7 (2010) 230–35.

Pinar, William. *What is Curriculum Theory?* Mahwah: Lawrence Erlbaum, 2004.

Pinar, William F., William M. Reynolds, Patrick Slattery, and Peter M. Taubman. *Understanding Curriculum: An Introduction to the Study of Historical and Contemporary Curriculum Discourses.* New York: Peter Lang, 1995.

Pink, Daniel H. *Pink: The Surprising Truth About What Motivates Us.* New York: Riverhead, 2009.

Popham, W. James. "Why Standardized Tests Don't Measure Educational Quality." *Educational Leadership* 56 (1999) 8–15.

Price, Todd Alan. "Teacher Education Under Audit: Value Added Measuring, TVAAS, EdTPA and Evidence-Based Theory." *Citizenship, Social and Economics Education* 13 (2014) 211–25.

Ravitch, Diane. *Reign of Error: The Hoax of the Privatization Movement and the Danger to America's Public Schools.* New York: Knopf, 2013.

Reeves, Douglas. "Level-Five Networks: Making Significant Change in Complex Organizations." In *Change Wars*, edited by Michael Barber et al., 237–256. Bloomington: Solution Tree, 2001.

Ryan, Frank X. *Seeing Together: Mind, Matter, and the Experimental Outlook of John Dewey and Arthur F. Bentley.* Great Barrington: American Institute for Economic Research, 2011.

Sahlberg, Pasi. *Finnish Lessons What Can the World Learn from Educational Change in Finland?* New York: Teachers College Press, 2011.

# Bibliography

Saltman, Kenneth. "The Rise of Venture Philanthropy and the Ongoing Neoliberal Assault on Public Education: The Eli and Edythe Broad Foundation." In *The Assault on Public Education: Confronting the Politics of Corporate School Reform,* edited by William H. Watkins, 55–78. New York: Teachers College Press, 2012.

Samford, Wendy L. "Deliberative Conversation: Cross-Paradigm Critique and Negotiation." In *Reconceptualizing Curriculum Development: Inspiring and Informing Action,* by James G. Henderson et al., 85–98. New York: Routledge, 2015.

———. "Exploring Sustained Change in Teachers' Beliefs After Professional Development." PhD diss., Kent State University, 2013.

Samford, Wendy L., Daniel J. Castner, Rosemary Gornik, James G. Henderson. "Teachers and Administrators as lead professionals for democratic ethics: From Course Design to Collaborative Journeys of Becoming." In *Theory of Educational Leadership as Curriculum Work: Toward a Comparative International Dialogue on Curriculum Theory and Leadership Research,* edited by Michael Uljens and Rose M. Ylimaki, New York: Springer, in press.

Samuels, Christina. "A Survey Detects Shifting Priorities of School Boards." *Education Week 30* (2011) 22.

Saunders-Smith, Gail. *The Ultimate Guided Reading How-To Book: Building Literacy Through Small-Group Instruction.* 2nd ed. Thousand Oaks: Corwin, 2009.

Sawchuk, Stephen. "NEA Proposes Making a Shift on Evaluation." *Education Week* 30 (2011) 18–9.

Schein, Edgar H. "Kurt Lewin's Change Theory in the Field and in the Classroom: Notes Toward a Model of Managed Learning." *Organizational Change* November 14, 2010, 1995.

Schubert, William H. "The Reconceptualization of Curriculum and Instruction." In *Curriculum Development in the Postmodern Era,* edited by Patrick Slattery, 56–57. New York: Garland, 1986.

Schwab, Joseph J. "The Practical: A Language for Curriculum." In *The Curriculum Studies Reader.* 2nd ed., edited by David J. Flinders and Stephen J. Thornton, 103–17. New York: Routledge, 2004.

———. *Science, Curriculum, and Liberal Education,* edited by Ian Westbury and Neil J. Wilkof, Chicago: The University of Chicago Press, 1978.

Schwandt, Thomas A. *Evaluation Practice Reconsidered.* New York: Peter Lang, 2002.

Schwartz, Barry, and Kenneth Sharpe. *Practical Wisdom: The Right Way to do the Right Thing.* New York: Penguin, 2010.

Short, Edmund C. *Forms of Curriculum Inquiry.* Albany: State University of New York Press, 1991.

Sirotnik, Kenneth A. "Making Sense of Educational Renewal." *Phi Delta Kappan 80* (1999) 606–10.

# Bibliography

Sister Mary Janet. "Life Adjustment: Open New Doors to Youth." *Educational Leadership* (December, 1954) 137–41.

Slattery, Patrick. *Curriculum Development in the Postmodern Era*. New York: Garland, 1995.

Smith, Christine, and Marilyn Gillespie. "Research on Professional Development and Teacher Change: Implications for Adult Basic Education." *Adult Learning and Literacy 7* (2007) 205–35.

Smith, Mary K. "Kurt Lewin: Groups, Experiential Learning and Action Research." *The Encyclopedia of Informal Education*, Last modified June 2001, http://www.infed.org/encyclopaedia.htm.

Smylie, Mark A., Sharon Conley, and Helen M. Marks. "Exploring New Approaches to Teacher Leadership for School Improvement." *The Educational Leadership Challenge: Redefining Leadership for the 21st Century*, 162–88. Chicago: University of Chicago Press, 2002.

Sousa, David A. *How the Brain Learns*. 3rd ed. Thousand Oaks: Corwin, 2006.

Spillane, James P. "Engaging practice: School Leadership and Management from a Distributed Perspective." In *Change Wars*, edited by Michael Barber et al., 201–19. Bloomington: Solution Tree, 2009.

Stumbo, Circe, and Peter McWalters. "Measuring Effectiveness: What Will It Take?" *Educational Leadership* 68 (2011) 10.

Taubman, Peter Maas. *Teaching by Numbers: Deconstructing the Discourse of Standards and Accountability in Education*. New York: Routledge, 2009.

Thomas, Wayne P., and Virginia P. Collier. *Dual Language for a Transformed World*. Albuquerque: Fuente, 2014.

Trejo, Shane. *North Dakota Action Alert: Help Ban Common Core, Support HB1461* (blog). *Tenth Amendment Center*, February 9, 2015. http://blog.tenthamendmentcenter.com/2015/02/north-dakota-action-alert-help-ban-common-core-support-hb1461/.

Tyler, Ralph W. *Basic Principles of Curriculum and Instruction*. Chicago: University of Chicago Press, 1949.

———. "Basic Principles of Curriculum and Instruction." In *The Curriculum Studies Reader*. 2nd ed., edited by David J. Flinders and Stephen J. Thornton, 51–9. New York: Routledge, 2004.

U.S. Department of Education. *Elementary and Secondary Education Act*. Accessed November 25, 2015. http://www.ed.gov/esea.

———. *A Nation at Risk*. Accessed November 24, 2015. http://www2.ed.gov/pubs/NatAtRisk/risk.html.

———. *Laws and Guidance/Elementary and Secondary Education*. Last modified March 12, 2014. http://www2.ed.gov/programs/elseccounseling/legislation.html.

———. *No Child Left Behind*. Accessed November 24, 2015. http://www2.ed.gov/nclb/landing.jhtml.

———. *The Secretary's Third Annual Report on Teacher Quality*. Jessup: Editorial Publications Center, 2004.

# BIBLIOGRAPHY

Walker, Decker F. "The Process of Curriculum Development: A Naturalistic Model." *School Review 80* (1971) 51–65.

Walker, Decker F., and Jonas F. Soltis. *Curriculum and Aims.* 5th ed. New York: Teachers College Press, 2009.

Watkins, William H. "The New Social Order: An Educator Looks at Economics, Politics, and Race." In *The Assault on Public Education: Confronting the Politics of Corporate School Reform,* edited by William H. Watkins, 7–32. New York: Teachers College Press, 2012.

———. *The Assault on Public Education: Confronting the Politics of Corporate School Reform.* New York: Teachers College Press, 2004.

Weber, Sandra J., and Claudia Mitchell. *That's Funny, You Don't Look Like a Teacher!: Interrogating Images, Identity, and Popular Culture.* Abingdon: Falmer, 1995.

Zull, James E. *The Art of Changing the Brain.* Sterling: Stylus, 2002.

Zhao, Yong. *Catching Up or Leading the Way: American Education in the Age of Globalization.* Alexandria: Association for Supervision and Curriculum Development, 2009.

www.ingramcontent.com/pod-product-compliance
Lightning Source LLC
Chambersburg PA
CBHW072144160426
43197CB00012B/2236